COLORADO
FARMERS' MARKET
COOKBOOK

Delicious Recipes & Tips *fresh*
from Colorado Farmers' Markets & Chefs

3D
PRESS

Colorado Farmers' Market Cookbook

First Edition

Design: Lisa and Marla Bachar
Cover Photography: Paul Bousquet

ISBN 1-889593-00-1

Printed in the United States

3D Press, Inc.
4340 E. Kentucky Ave., Suite 446
Denver, CO 80246
303-300-4484 (phone)
303-300-4494 (fax)
info@3dpress.net

888-456-3607 (order toll-free)
www.3dpress.net

Foreword

Every summer morning, as the first rays of sunlight illuminate the peaks of the Rockies, farm trucks, filled to overflowing, lumber slowly into their spaces at any one of Colorado's 63 farmers' markets. While the city is still sleeping, market tents spring up, tables are unfolded and banners hung. Boxes and bushel baskets are unloaded and beautiful table displays created. Farmers put the finishing touches on their stands and prepare for the questions that are sure to come: When were these picked? ... Is this a good variety for canning? ... What is the best way to use these?

It's true that goodwill comes easily at the market, and it naturally follows that new friendships are formed each week. Farmers' markets provide a 'feel good' experience for everyone who takes part. Do a little people watching the next time you're at the Market. You'll notice conversations springing up in every nook and cranny. And you'll see vendors remembering the names of customers from the week before.

Farmers' Markets are a boon to the every cook, whether novice or professional. Anyone can appreciate quality and freshness – and Markets offer the freshest, most flavorful fruits and vegetables available. Produce is typically picked the night before or the morning of the market. Because the varieties are grown for flavor, and not for shipping or storage qualities, you'll find tomatoes that taste like tomatoes, peaches that are juicy and delicious, the sweetest corn on the cob and apricots that have been picked ripe from the tree.

Though fruits and vegetables form the foundation of the farmers' markets, other local producers are just as much a part of the experience. Ranchers bring their naturally raised beef and buffalo. And farmers bring free-range chickens and fresh brown and white eggs. Local beekeepers share their beautiful honeys and bee's wax products. There are cheeses for every palate and every menu. Salsas, mustards and chutneys share space with fresh pasta and chili and soup mixes. And don't forget the just roasted chiles and the Western Slope cider, fruit juices, syrups, dried fruits and jams.

Whether you only have recently chosen to shop at a farmers' market, or you are a seasoned veteran, please know that supporting the markets is a choice that matters. Not only for yourself and your family, but also for your community and the state. Farmers' markets provide a place for food producers to sell directly to the public, so that they can earn a living wage and continue to farm the beautiful open spaces that we all love and desire to preserve.

People don't become farmers to get rich, that's for certain. But your encouragement and smiling faces each week help them to remember that what they do is important and that it is greatly appreciated by so many. Every purchase you make sends a statement that local agriculture and family farms and businesses are a vital part of Colorado's past, present and future.

Laura Korth, President, Colorado Farmers' Market Association

Introduction

Farmers' markets and roadside stands selling fresh, local produce and specialty foods thrive in Colorado. Colorado residents and visitors are discovering the allure of the markets and the joys of cooking with farm fresh ingredients. Over one million people visit Colorado farmers' markets each year, enjoying the state's exceptional fruits and vegetables, natural meats, hand-made cheeses, specialty foods and so much more.

The *Colorado Farmers' Market Cookbook* captures the essence and spirit of these markets. Whether you are just discovering the the markets, or are an expert at incorporating Colorado's bounty into your cooking, this book is a great resource.

Once you have tried a Palisade peach, blue cheese from Fort Collins' Bingham Hill or organic basil from Boulder's Burke Farms, you will recognize the exceptional quality of products that are hand-raised or hand-made with taste, rather shelf-life, in mind.

More and more, home cooks and professional chefs alike are recognizing the taste *and* health benefits of incorporating fresh, natural seasonal ingredients into their cooking. In this book, you will find a wide variety of recipes that focus on the flavors of the ingredients.

The *Colorado Farmers' Market Cookbook* has over 175 recipes from Colorado farmers, ranchers and specialty food producers, as well as some of Colorado's leading chefs, who feature seasonal menus using locally grown products. It also includes 21 entertaining articles, filled with information about different products, along with suggestions for how to choose, store and prepare each one.

Cooking tips are sprinkled throughout the book, and in the back, you will find a handy guide and map to the state's farmers' markets and contact information for all of the featured farmers, ranchers, food festivals and specialty food producers.

The *Colorado Farmers' Market Cookbook* will inspire an appreciation for Colorado's abundance of delicious local fruits, vegetables, meats, cheeses and specialty foods. Cooking with fresh, local foods is a win/win proposition. You benefit by eating healthier, tastier meals, and at the same time you are supporting Colorado farmers, ranchers and specialty food producers.

Remember, even the simplest recipe can be sensational when made with the best ingredients!

TABLE OF CONTENTS

ARTICLE INDEX

About the Authors

Melissa Craven brings her love of the written word and her love for cooking to the task of compiling and editing this book. Melissa has a background in journalism, marketing and public relations. As a writer, she is tireless in her quest for clear, concise prose. As a cook, she understands the sheer joy that comes from creating memorable meals for family and friends. Her melding of the two help create a winning recipe.

Janis B. Judd, CCP is a well-respected culinary authority in her hometown of Boulder, Colorado. A self-taught cook, Judd has spent over 30 years honing her skills with such culinary legends as Giuliano Bugialli, Lynne Rossetto Kasper, Richard Grausman and Madeleine Kamman in both the U.S. and France. In 1998, Judd earned the designation of Certified Culinary Professional (CCP) from the International Association of Culinary Professionals. Judd also holds degrees in nursing and business. Judd is the author of *Boulder Cooks*, which won Best How-to Book from the Rocky Mountain Book Publishers Association in 1997. Judd has also competed in and served as a judge for cooking competitions In 1997, her apple pie took second place at the National Pie Championship.

Laura Korth is president of the Colorado Farmers' Market Association. She is also the founder and director of the Longmont Farmers' Market. She is a frequent contributor to the Longmont Daily Times-Call with her seasonal column, *At The Market*. Laura has been trained and certified as a Master Food Preserver through CSU Cooperative Extension. She currently serves as a member of the Boulder County Cooperative Extension Advisory Board for the area of Food Safety. She frequently speaks and teaches on topics relating to farmers' markets, food safety and seasonal cooking.

Before Beginning

Before beginning to prepare a recipe from this book, please review the following information. It will help you achieve the best results. You may also want to refer to it for certain recipes.

In general, be sure to carefully read all the way through a recipe before preparing it the first time. Have all the ingredients, as well as utensils and other needed equipment, ready before you begin. It will save time and confusion if you do as much advance preparation as possible.

A word about ingredients:
It goes without saying that the better the quality of the ingredients, the better the results will be. In this cookbook we do not specify, for example, "extra virgin olive oil, first cold press" each time olive oil is called for, or "freshly ground black pepper" each time pepper is used.

Ingredients:
Butter – when butter is called for, we mean salted butter. Unsalted butter is specified if required. If you substitute margarine, be aware that the results will be different.

Zest – this is the colored part of the skin of citrus fruit. The zest is removed with a vegetable peeler and minced, or removed with a zester. Before removing the zest, wash the fruit thoroughly and dry it. Use only the colored part of the skin, not the bitter white pith underneath.

Methods:
This book assumes you have a knowledge of common kitchen practices and good hygiene, such as hand washing, rinsing chicken and other foods before using them and refrigerating perishables. If a recipe calls for a change in common procedures, it is specified in the text.

Blanching – plunge food into boiling water for a brief period (10 to 15 seconds) and then place it in a bowl of ice water. This process heightens color and flavor. It also helps loosen the skin to make peeling easier for certain nuts, fruits, and vegetables.

Corn – to get the kernels off an ear of corn, use a knife and, using a sawing motion, go down the length of a cob, cut away about one-half to two-thirds of the kernels, leaving the base. After you have cut all the way around the cob, go back with the dull edge of the knife. Push hard down the sides of the cob to push out the remaining "meat" of the corn and its milk.

Hot chiles – the utmost care should be taken when handling hot chiles. Chiles exude an oil that stays on anything it touches. Wash everything that has come in contact with cut chiles: the knife, the cutting board and, most especially, your hands. If you are especially sensitive, use rubber gloves. (Contact lens wearers should be especially careful. Scrub your hands with salt and then with soap to remove the chile oils before touching his eyes or lenses.) As a general rule, remove the white, spongy ribs and the seeds from chiles before chopping them. These parts contain the greatest concentration of capsaicin, the compound that makes chiles hot.

Peeling peaches – plunge peaches into boiling water for about 10 or 15 seconds, depending on the ripeness of the peach. Remove and allow to cool. The skin should come off easily.

Peeling tomatoes – plunge tomatoes into boiling water for about 5 seconds and remove immediately. The skin should slip off easily.

Pumpkin purée - to extract pumpkin from a fresh pumpkin: cut the pumpkin in half and place cut side-down on a baking sheet. Roast in a 350°F oven for about 30 minutes, until the flesh of the pumpkin is tender. Remove from the oven and let cool. Scrape out the flesh and purée the pumpking in a blender or food processor or mash it.

Roasting and peeling peppers – there are many ways to roast and peel peppers. One method is to line a baking sheet with foil and preheat the broiler. Put the peppers in a single layer on the baking sheet and broil for 3 to 4 minutes, then turn them. Continue broiling and turning the peppers until all sides are blistered and slightly charred but not black. Immediately seal the peppers in a brown paper bag to steam them. After 10 or 15 minutes, remove the peppers. The peppers should now peel easily under running water. Remove the skin and seeds, and prepare the peppers according to the recipe. Other methods of peeling a pepper include holding the pepper over the flame of a gas stove or placing it directly on the grill.

About cooking at high altitude:
The recipes in this book have been tested at an altitude of approximately 5,200 feet. If you live at a significantly higher or lower altitude, you may want to adjust the amounts of certain ingredients and the cooking or baking times.

For every 1,000 foot increase in altitude from sea level, water boils at a temperature two degrees lower. In Denver, water boils at 203°F compared to 212°F at sea level. At higher altitude allow a little more time when cooking in water. At lower altitude watch that food doesn't overcook. A rule of thumb is to boil foods four percent longer per each 1,000 feet gained and four percent shorter per each 1,000 feet lost. Baking or roasting also takes less time at low altitude; check for doneness five to 10 minutes earlier than the time specified in the recipe.

When baking at high altitude, use slightly less sugar, shortening or butter, baking powder and yeast, and more egg white, cream of tartar, liquid, and flour. Do the opposite at low altitude. Since water evaporates faster at high altitude, baked goods may need more liquid. Increase the liquid in the dough or batter by teaspoons until you get the proper texture. The baking powder in cookie recipes should be increased and the sugar slightly decreased when prepared at a higher altitude. At low altitude, the opposite is true in each case (except do not increase the sugar). There are differing opinions as to the exact amount of this and that to add or subtract when you are changing a recipe which has been tested at an altitude different from yours. Understanding the effects of higher altitude and experimenting will help you more than anything.

SALSAS, SAUCES & CONDIMENTS

Pumpkin Dog Treats

Pam Osborn, of Osborn Farms, says, "Our dogs are always eating pumpkins, so we came up with these doggie treats." Our dog biscuit tester, Roger (photo on right), picks these biscuits over store-bought every time!

*Makes
24 biscuits*

2	cups whole wheat flour
¼	cup cornmeal
⅓	cup flour
1	teaspoon salt
2	tablespoons vegetable oil
¼	cup dark molasses
2	eggs
¼	cup milk
1	cup rolled oats
1	cup cooked, puréed pumpkin (or use canned pumpkin)

Preheat the oven to 350°F. Mix all of the ingredients together. Roll out the mixture on a floured surface. Cut into shapes (use a pumpkin or dog-shaped cookie cutter) and put on a baking sheet. Bake for 30 minutes. Turn off the oven and leave the biscuits in the oven to cool (this makes them crunchier).

Courtesy of Osborn Farm

Fresh Honey Lemonade

César Flores produces honey and bee hive products such as honey comb, bee pollen, royal jelly, honey wine vinegar, beeswax skin cream and lip balm, and this honey lemonade, which is very popular at farmers' markets in July and August.

Makes 2 quarts

2	cups hot water
1	cup local honey
1½	cups lemon juice (at least 10 ripe, organic lemons)
1½	quarts (6 cups) cold spring water

Combine the hot water and honey; stir until the honey is blended into the water. Combine the honey mixture, lemon juice and spring water in a pitcher. Adjust quantities to taste. Pour into tall, frosted, ice-filled glasses and garnish with a sprig of mint and/or a lemon slice.

Courtesy of César Flores, Beekeeper

Honey Cranberry Relish

Joe and JoAnne Erickson started J&J Apiaries in 1990 as a hobby. In 1992, they retired and expanded the apiary into a sideline business. Working with bees has proven to be an enjoyable craft for the Ericksons. They produce honey, beeswax candles and crafts. You can find their products at farmers' markets and holiday shows. Besides being perfect for Thanksgiving dinner, this relish is perfect with Honey Pepper Pork Roast (see page 150).

Makes 2¼ cups

1	medium orange, washed and dried
1	10-ounce package fresh or frozen cranberries
¾	cup honey

Quarter and slice the unpeeled orange, then squeeze out the seeds. Coarsely chop the unpeeled orange and the cranberries; put them in a medium saucepan. Stir in the honey and bring the mixture to a boil over medium heat. Cook for 3 to 4 minutes. Cool and serve.

Courtesy of J&J Apiaries

Homemade Applesauce

"In the autumn months, our breakfasts frequently feature apples in one form or another," says Laura Korth of the Colorado Farmers' Market Association and the Longmont Farmers' Market. We use a lot of homemade applesauce in breakfast items such as muffins, quick breads, breakfast bars and as a topping for pancakes. If you've never made applesauce, this is an easy one to start with." Braeburn, Granny Smith, McIntosh, Jonagold and Rome are some good varieties to use in this recipe. The texture should be slightly chunky. The optional butter adds depth and richness to the sauce, and helps prevent sticking during cooking.

Serves
2 to 4

4	mildly tart apples, washed, peeled, quartered and cored
1	teaspoon lemon juice
⅛	teaspoon salt
1	tablespoon butter (optional)
1½	tablespoons brown sugar, or more to taste (optional)
¼	teaspoon cinnamon (optional)

Thinly slice the apples and put them in a large saucepan. Add the lemon juice, butter and sugar. Cover and cook over low heat for 15 to 20 minutes, stirring occasionally, until the apples are very soft. Remove from the heat and mash the apples with a potato masher or fork (the texture should be slightly chunky). Stir in the cinnamon, if desired. Serve warm or cold.

Courtesy of Laura Korth, Longmont Farmers' Market

Tomatillo Salsa

Tomatillos are small, green Mexican tomatoes. If you have never tried them, this salsa is a great introduction to this tangy fruit. It's very easy to make and everyone loves the flavor. Choose tomatillos that are firm to the touch with their papery husks intact.

Makes
2 cups

1	pound tomatillos, papery husks removed, washed and chopped
½	cup minced onion
¼	cup chopped cilantro
1	medium tomato, chopped
1	mild chile (such as Anaheim or poblano), seeded and chopped
2	jalapeño or serrano chiles, seeded and minced
1	tablespoon lime juice
1	teaspoon olive oil
½	teaspoon salt

Combine all of the ingredients and refrigerate for at least 1 hour (and up to 3 days) for the flavors to blend. Serve with tortilla chips.

Courtesy of Buckskin Trail Gardens

Basil

Just how many varieties of basil are there? Good question – I've lost count in recent years. But one thing is certain: if there is a variety to be tried, you'll find it at the farmers' market.

Varietal differences are seen in the size and texture of the leaf, the scent, the color or the depth of flavor. You can't go wrong with any variety, but it's fun to be able to try several and see which ones work best in your favorite dishes.

Fresh basil, stored in a plastic bag, will last up to a week in the crisper drawer of the refrigerator. It can be used in so many dishes, it's impossible to list them all here.

One thing customers at the markets say they like to do with fresh basil is to lay whole leaves over sliced tomatoes, top with fresh buffalo mozzarella cheese, then drizzle with extra virgin olive oil or a light vinaigrette for a simple *Insalata Caprese*.

Or, layer the same ingredients (without the dressing) on a slice of crusty French bread that has been rubbed with a cut garlic clove, then run it under the broiler to soften the cheese for a really great open-faced sandwich.

Basil can be preserved for winter with nothing more than a little string. Wash the basil and gently pat it dry. Put a few stems together in a bunch and tie a piece of string around the end of the stems. Hang the herbs upside down in a cool place for about a week. How quickly the leaves dry will depend on the level of humidity at the time. When dry, run your hand down the stems to dislodge the leaves and put them in a jar with a tight-fitting lid.

To use dried basil in a recipe, crush the amount you need in your palm. This unlocks the essential oils in the basil and the wonderful aroma that was trapped inside comes bursting forth. Add the basil to your recipe at the end of the cooking time for the best flavor. In general, you need one-third less dried basil than fresh. In other words, 1 teaspoon crushed dried basil = 1 tablespoon chopped fresh basil.

Perfect Pesto / Makes About 2 Cups

Chris and Michele Burke, owners of Burke Organic Farms and the Colorado Fresh Markets, are part of a resurgence of people interested in preserving the quality of our land, food and environment. They are forgoing traditional jobs to become small farmers. The Burkes produce cut greens, arugula, basil, spinach, garlic, an assortment of seasonal vegetables and 59 varieties of heirloom and hybrid tomatoes. They sell the majority of their produce and flowers at Denver and Boulder farmers' markets. For the Burke's pesto, experiment with the quantities until you find the perfect taste and consistency. Toss the pesto with pasta or serve it as a condiment for chicken, meat or fish. Leftover pesto can be stored for up to one week in the refrigerator or frozen for later use.

4   cups Burke organic basil
4   cloves Burke organic garlic, or more to taste
1   cup walnuts, pine nuts or pistachios
1   cup extra virgin olive oil, or more if needed
1   cup freshly grated Reggiano Parmesan cheese
Salt

Put the basil, garlic, nuts and olive oil in a blender or food processor and process until creamy (or blend less for a coarser sauce). Add more oil if the sauce seems too thick. Add the cheese and pulse just to blend. Add salt to taste.

Article courtesy of Laura Korth, Longmont Farmers' Market; Recipe courtesy of Burke Organic Farms

Roasted Green Chile Salsa

This is a simple and tasty roasted salsa, with chile heat to your taste.

Makes
2 cups

6	tomatoes, peeled and chopped
1-2	roasted chiles (hot, mild or a mix), peeled, seeded and chopped
1	small onion, chopped
1	clove garlic, minced

Juice of ½ lime

2	tablespoons chopped cilantro

Salt

Combine all the ingredients in a bowl and let sit for 1 hour to blend the flavors.

Courtesy of Monroe Organic Farms

Summer Italian Tomato Sauce

Established in 1936 to sell produce to grocery stores, Monroe Organic Farms is now a Community Supported Agriculture project supporting 250 households. Along with produce, the Monroes raise organic beef, chicken and eggs. This sauce can be stored in the refrigerator in airtight glass or plastic container for one week.

Makes
2 cups

8	tomatoes, peeled and coarsely chopped
1	large onion, chopped
2-3	cloves garlic, minced
1½	tablespoons chopped fresh oregano
1½	tablespoons chopped fresh basil
1	teaspoon sugar
½	teaspoon salt
½	teaspoon black pepper

Purée the tomatoes, onion and garlic in a food processor or blender. Transfer the mixture to a 6-quart saucepan. Add the oregano, basil, sugar, salt and pepper. Bring to a boil, reduce the heat, cover and simmer for 20 minutes. Uncover the pan, stir and simmer until the sauce has thickened, about 15 to 20 minutes. Season to taste with salt and pepper.

Courtesy of Monroe Organic Farms

Pizza Sauce

If you are not using this pizza sauce immediately, it can be frozen or canned. The Colorado State University Cooperative Extension has clear, simple instructions for safe canning. For directions, call the your local Extension office and ask for Fact Sheet #9341, or look on-line at www.ext.colostate.edu/pubs/foodnut/09341.html.

Makes
4 cups

¼	cup olive oil
½	small onion, chopped
2	cloves garlic, minced
10	cups peeled and chopped Roma tomatoes
¼	cup sugar
1	tablespoon chopped fresh basil, or 1 teaspoon dried
1	tablespoon chopped fresh oregano, or 1 teaspoon dried
1	tablespoon chopped fresh parsley
3	bay leaves
1	tablespoon fennel seed

Heat the olive oil in a large saucepan over medium heat. Add the onions and cook until they are soft. Add the garlic and stir for 1 minute. Remove the pan from the heat.

Purée the tomatoes in a blender or food processor. Strain the purée through a sieve or food mill, then add it to the onion mixture. Add the sugar, basil, oregano and parsley; mix well. Stir in the bay leaves and fennel seed. Return the mixture to the stove. Cook over medium heat until the sauce reaches the desired thickness, about 3 to 4 hours.

Courtesy of Mattics Orchards

Creating a Great Cheese Course

Most of us think of cheese as part of a sandwich or as intensely orange bricks. But there is so much more to discover about cheese! Here are Bingham Hill Cheese Company's recommendations for a five-senses experience with cheese:

1. Select three artisanal cheeses using a theme:
   a. the same family (all blues, all hard, all bloomy rind)
   b. the same geographic region (all Colorado, all California, all Vermont)
   c. different milks (sheep, goat, cow, water buffalo, etc.)
   d. different finishes (unaged, washed, bloomy rind and very aged)
   e. different categories (soft, semi-soft, hard)

2. A cheese course is best served as an appetizer, before dessert or as dessert after a light dinner, although it is great for lunch as well.

3. As with wine, it is best to try different cheeses from mild to flavorful, unless you already know which ones are your favorites!

4. Cut the serving portions 30 minutes before serving. Wrap both the to-be-served portions and the to-be-stored portions and leave the to-be-served portions out to reach room temperature. Refrigerate the remainder.

5. When serving, place one wedge of each cheese (don't cut into chunks, it will dry out) on as many dark-colored dishes as will serve four. The dark colors offset and define the light-colored cheeses. Place dark-colored dried fruit, such as figs or dates, or nuts on a light-colored plate to achieve the same effect. Place a sharp knife (a paring knife works well) with each cheese. Serve with crusty bread and wine.

6. A note about wine and cheese: a great cheese will bolster an acceptable wine, but a bad cheese can ruin even the best wine. When thinking about wine and cheese pairings, think back to your high-school chemistry class. Is the cheese rich? Try an acidic wine. Is the cheese acidic? Try a sweet wine. Is the cheese powerful? Try a beer or a bold wine. However, don't get stuck on what the experts say should go with a particular cheese. For instance, late-harvest Rieslings are delicious with blues, even though port has been promoted as a blue companion.

7. Lastly, relax and take time to smell, feel, see, taste and hear the cheese!

Courtesy of Kristi Johnson, Bingham Hill Cheese Company

APPETIZERS

Sirloin Steak Bruschetta

This quick and easy dish is a tasty way to use your fresh herbs and tomatoes. Serve it as an appetizer, using thin baguette slices, or serve it as a sandwich using thicker slices of fresh rustic bread. Try flavoring the bread with garlic butter and grilling it. If you have time, marinate the tomatoes for one to two hours – it will really enhance their flavor.

Serves 4

1 pound Coleman Natural top sirloin steak
Coarsely ground black pepper
2 cloves garlic, minced
1⅓ cups peeled and chopped Roma tomatoes
2 tablespoons chopped fresh basil
1 tablespoon balsamic vinegar
2 teaspoons olive oil
½ stick butter, at room temperature
1 French baguette, thinly sliced
4 tablespoons crumbled feta cheese

Season the steak generously with freshly ground black pepper and one-third of the minced garlic. Let the steak sit, covered, for 30 minutes to absorb the flavor. Grill or broil the steak to your taste. Let the steak sit for 5 minutes off the heat and then slice it 1-inch thick.

In a small bowl, combine the tomatoes, basil, vinegar, oil and one-third of the minced garlic. Cover and set aside.

Mash the butter with the remaining third of the minced garlic. Spread the garlic butter on one side of each baguette slice and grill them on the buttered side.

Place the grilled bread on a serving plate. Top each slice of bread with steak, some of the tomato mixture and a sprinkle of cheese. Serve open-face, or top with another baguette slice to make little sandwiches.

Courtesy of Coleman Natural Products

Goat Cheese-Stuffed Portobello Mushrooms

This is a nice appetizer any time of year. It can also be served with couscous and sautéed vegetables as a vegetarian meal.

Serves 4

3-4 large portobello mushroom caps
Balsamic vinaigrette (see page 42)
4-6 ounces Haystack Mountain herbed goat cheese
1 cup Italian herbed bread crumbs
Extra virgin olive oil
4 cups mixed field greens

Preheat the oven to 400°F. Wipe the tops of the mushrooms with a wet paper towel to clean them. Carve out the gills on the underside, then brush them with balsamic vinaigrette. Slice the goat cheese and divide it among the mushrooms, placing it inside the mushroom caps. Sprinkle with the bread crumbs. Spray or drizzle the mushrooms with olive oil and place them on a baking sheet on the top rack of the oven. Bake the mushrooms for 5 to 8 minutes, until the mushrooms are sizzling and the cheese starts to melt. Broil the mushrooms if additional browning is desired. Remove the mushrooms to a cutting board and quarter them. Divide the field greens among 4 plates and top with the mushrooms. Splash with additional vinaigrette, if desired, and serve.

Courtesy of Chef Mick Rosacci, Tony's Meats & Specialty Foods

Cheese-Stuffed Chiles

Located east of Pueblo, the St. Charles Mesa, with its warm, dry summers, fertile soil and pure water, is the ideal "hot spot" for growing chiles. Pueblo chiles are moderately hot chiles known as Mirasol ("Mirasol" means facing the sun in Spanish), because they grow with their tips facing up. The cream cheese in this recipe cuts the fire of the chiles but still preserves their unique flavor. Serve these jazzy nibbles as an appetizer or as a garnish for green salads.

Serves 6

12 Pueblo chiles
6 ounces regular or light cream cheese, more or less depending on the size of the chiles

Slit the chiles down one side, seed them and remove the white membranes. Stuff each chile with cream cheese, pull the sides together and serve.

Courtesy of Pueblo Farmers Marketeers

Sweet and Sour Elk Meatballs

Two of the largest elk ranches in Colorado (Prock Elk Ranch of Montrose and Anta Grande Elk Ranch of Del Norte) are owned by the late Wanda Prock's children. These meatballs were a favorite recipe of Wanda's. It is a delicious appetizer with just the right balance of sweet and tangy.

Serves
4 to 6

2	pounds ground elk
1	cup rolled oats
2	eggs
½	medium onion, chopped
1½	teaspoons plus 1 tablespoon Worcestershire sauce
2	tablespoons butter, at room temperature
¾	cup packed dark brown sugar
⅓	cup cider vinegar
1	teaspoon yellow mustard
⅓	cup barbecue sauce
2	tablespoons chopped fresh chives

Salt and black pepper

Preheat the oven to 350°F. Mix the elk, oats, eggs, onion and 1½ teaspoons Worcestershire. Form the mixture into 1-inch diameter meatballs. Melt the butter in a skillet and cook the meatballs in the butter until browned.

To make the sauce, combine the sugar, vinegar, mustard, barbecue sauce, chives and 1 tablespoon Worcestershire. Season with salt and pepper. Place the meatballs in a shallow baking dish. Pour the sauce over the meatballs and toss to coat. Bake for 30 minutes. Serve with toothpicks to stab the meatballs.

Courtesy of Anta Grande Premium Elk Meat

Brushcetta of Goat Cheese, Peaches, Roasted Red Pepper and Basil

The inspiration for the Denver restaurant Potager comes from a father and daughter team who share a love of excellent food. Their goal is to serve "really satisfying food," using the best seasonal ingredients. Each week, they shop local farmers' markets and farms for the best organic foods. It is their appreciation for using the freshest ingredients in unique and creative ways that makes dining at Potager an exceptional experience.

Serves 4

1	sourdough baguette, thinly sliced
	Olive oil
2	red bell peppers
2	peaches, peeled, halved and pitted
2	tablespoons chopped fresh basil
2	tablespoons sugar
3	tablespoons balsamic vinegar
6	ounces goat cheese, at room temperature

Preheat the oven to 325°F. Brush the baguette slices on both sides with olive oil and place directly on the oven rack. Toast until dry, but not browning.

Roast the red peppers over an open flame until blackened and blistered all over. Seal in a paper bag and let cool. Under cold, running water, peel the charred skins, then seed the peppers and cut them into strips.

Bring the sugar and balsamic vinegar to a boil in a saucepan. Remove the pan from the heat and cool. Spread some goat cheese on each toasted baguette slices. Top with peach slices, roasted red pepper and a little chopped basil. Drizzle with balsamic syrup and serve.

Courtesy of Potager

Sweet and Sour Veggies

This a perfect snack for junk-food addicts. It satisfies your craving for sweets while putting a few vitamins in your diet. The recipe could also be served as a salad or side dish. It will keep in the refrigerator for up to a week.

Makes
8 cups

2	cups broccoli florets
1	medium red bell pepper, thinly sliced
1	medium green bell pepper, thinly sliced
3	stalks celery, sliced
8	large mushrooms, quartered
1	small head cauliflower, separated into florets
1	small onion, thinly sliced
2	teaspoons salt
1	cup sugar
½	cup distilled white vinegar
1	cup olive oil
2	teaspoons poppy seeds

Put the broccoli, bell peppers, celery, mushrooms, cauliflower and onion in a plastic or crockery container with a tight-fitting lid. Combine the salt, sugar, vinegar, oil and poppy seeds in a jar and shake to mix well. Pour the vinegar mixture over the vegetables and toss to coat. Cover and refrigerate for at least 3 hours before serving. Serve chilled.

Courtesy of Pueblo Farmers Marketeers

Dilly Beans and Carrots

R&K Farms, founded in 1997, operates on the belief that farm fresh products should be available to the general public at reasonable prices, "even in the twenty-first century." R&K Farms is "your farm in the city" – they do all the work and will even deliver. The farm offers seasonal vegetables, eggs and poultry, and beef, pork and lamb to order. The beans and carrots in this recipe can be served as a starter to munch on, or as a relish. They will keep, refrigerated, for several weeks.

Serves
6 to 8

2	cups distilled white vinegar
¼	cup honey
1	teaspoon dill weed
1	teaspoon pickling spice blend
1	clove garlic, crushed
½	cup water

1   tablespoon salt
4   medium carrots, peeled and cut into ¼-inch sticks
12 fresh green beans, ends snapped off

In a large saucepan, combine the vinegar, honey, dill, pickling spice, garlic, water and salt. Bring the mixture to a boil over medium-high heat. Add the carrots and beans. Reduce the heat to low and simmer for 10 minutes. Let cool, then refrigerate for 3 to 4 hours before serving.

Courtesy of R&K Farms

Goat Cheese Spread with Pecans and Fresh Herbs

Haystack Mountain Goat Dairy offers chèvre (goat cheese), plain or flavored with ingredients like Herbes de Provence, rosemary, cracked pepper, dill, sun-dried tomatoes, garlic and green chiles. They now also produce traditional goat milk feta cheese. Look for Haystack cheese at many farmer's markets around Colorado and check out their website (www.haystackgoatcheese.com) for a look at the dairy. This spread is simple to prepare. The fresh taste of herbs, with a little punch (from cayenne) and crunch (from pecans), makes a savory starter.

Makes
1½ cups

3   tablespoons minced parsley
1   tablespoon chopped chives
1   small clove garlic, minced
12 ounces Haystack Chèvre, or other goat cheese, at room temperature
2   tablespoons olive oil
¼   teaspoon paprika
¼   teaspoon ground cumin
⅛   teaspoon cayenne pepper
¼   teaspoon freshly ground black pepper
2   tablespoons chopped pecans
1   French baguette, sliced and toasted

Purée the parsley, chives and garlic in a food processor or blender. Add the goat cheese, olive oil, paprika, cumin, cayenne and black pepper. Purée until blended and smooth. Add the pecans and pulse a few times to combine, but not pulverize. Transfer the mixture to a crock or serving bowl. Serve at room temperature with toasted baguette slices.

Courtesy of Haystack Mountain Goat Dairy

Crispy Polenta with Grilled Pears in Gorgonzola Cream

Boulder native Bradford Heap is co-owner and chef of Boulder's acclaimed Full Moon Grill. He changes the menu often, planning around seasonal vegetables and fruits. Heap's food demonstrates the influences of his work and studies at the Culinary Institute of America and in Europe. This is one of his favorite appetizers. Comice or Bosc pears are the best choices for this recipe. They should be ripe and unblemished. If you are peeling the pears, but are not cooking them right away, rub them with a little fresh lemon juice to prevent them from turning brown. The polenta can be made up to two days ahead. If you don't have time to make it, you can buy tubes of pre-made polenta in most grocery stores. A cookie cutter works well for cutting the polenta.

Serves 4

1	medium onion, finely minced
2	tablespoons extra virgin olive oil
1	cup polenta
4	cups water
½	teaspoon salt

Canola oil

½	cup heavy cream
4½	ounces Gorgonzola cheese, plus more as needed
2	medium pears, halved and cored
2	ounces pine nuts, toasted

Chopped Italian parsley to garnish
Chopped red bell pepper to garnish

Preheat the oven to 350°F. Place the onion and olive oil in an oven-proof saucepan and cover. Cook the onions over low heat for about 5 minutes, until tender but not browned. Add the polenta and stir for 1 minute. Add the water and salt to taste. Bring to a boil, stirring constantly. Immediately remove the pan from the heat and cover.

Place the pan in the oven and bake for about 1 hour, stirring after 30 minutes. The mixture should be smooth. Grease a 10x10-inch baking dish and pour the polenta into it. Smooth the top and let it cool. The polenta can be made to this point up to 2 days in advance.

Cut the polenta into 8 small rounds, squares or triangles. Heat a little canola oil in a skillet, until the oil is almost smoking. Add the polenta rounds to the pan and sear each side until golden brown.

To make the sauce, heat the cream to boiling, then transfer it to a blender along with the Gorgonzola. Blend until smooth. If the mixture seems too thin, add more Gorgonzola to thicken it.

Cut a 45-degree angle slice from the back of each pear half so they will sit up on the plate. Lightly brush each pear half with canola oil and grill (or bake at 400°F) until heated through (be careful not to overcook the pears or they will get mushy).

To serve, put a little sauce on a warm plate. Place 2 rounds of pan-fried polenta on the bottom part of the plate and place one grilled pear half at the top. Sprinkle with pine nuts and serve. For more color, sprinkle with chopped Italian parsley and/or a small amount of chopped red bell pepper.

Courtesy of Full Moon Grill

Cherry Tomatoes with Pesto

Loredana's Pesto got its start in 1993 at the Downtown Denver Farmers' Market. "I borrowed some crates and an old door from the farmers and made a table," Loredana says. "I sold out my first batch of pesto in an hour, and have been making it ever since." This is a simple, healthy appetizer that is at its best in spring and summer. Loredana's Casalinga Pesto is a classic pesto. Durango Pesto is a spicy pesto with cilantro and jalapeño.

Serves
8 to 10

1   pound cherry tomatoes (about 36 tomatoes)
1   6.5-ounce container Loredana's Casalinga or
     Durango Pesto, or other favorite pesto
Fresh basil leaves for garnish

Wash the tomatoes and slice off the top of each. Carefully scoop out the seeds with the small end of a melon baller or other small spoon. Fill each tomato with pesto. Chill for 1 hour. To serve, arrange the tomatoes on a plate and garnish with fresh basil leaves.

Courtesy of Loredana's Pesto

Eggplant Almond Pâté

Eden Valley Organic Farm is where "nutritious meets delicious." Luscious red raspberries, juicy fresh tomatoes, crispy sweet peppers and deep purple eggplants are just a few of the quality vegetables and fruits Eden Valley farm produces. The flavor of the eggplant in this recipe is enhanced with toasted almonds. Even if you are not an eggplant lover, give this recipe a try – it has changed many people's feelings about the vegetable.

Makes
2 cups

1	cup raw almonds
4-5	small Asian eggplants (or 1 large eggplant), peeled and chopped
4	cloves garlic, minced
1	tablespoon chopped fresh thyme or marjoram
¾	cup chopped mushrooms
1	medium onion, chopped
1	teaspoon seasoning salt or sea salt
½	cup water

Preheat the oven to 350°F. Put the almonds on a cookie sheet and toast in the oven for 8 to 10 minutes, until light brown. Let the almonds cool, then put them in a blender or food processor and process until finely ground. Leave the almonds in the blender.

Place the eggplant, garlic, thyme, mushrooms, onion and salt in a wok or large skillet. Add ¼ cup of water and simmer, stirring occasionally, until the vegetables are tender and the water has been absorbed.

Gradually add ¼ cup of water to the almonds in the blender and process until a paste is made. Add the eggplant mixture and blend until smooth. Thoroughly chill the pâté. Serve the pâté on a bed of lettuce surrounded with pita bread, crackers or thinly sliced French bread.

Courtesy of Eden Valley Farms

Tomato Salsa with Garlic Toasts

Munson Farms was started in 1976 by Bob and Marcy Munson. The Munsons specialize in sweet corn and pumpkins. They also offer a wide variety of vegetables including spinach and other greens, sugar peas, tomatoes, zucchini, melons, squash and herbs. The Munsons participate in several Colorado farmers' markets and have their own stand, which is open from July through October. Munson Farms created this recipe using their vine-ripened tomatoes and fresh basil. It's very easy to put together and is a perfect appetizer when tomatoes are at their peak.

For the garlic butter:

Serves 8

2	cloves garlic, chopped
1	large shallot, chopped
1	stick butter, at room temperature

Salt and black pepper

Put the garlic and shallot in a food processor and pulse a few times. Add the butter and process until smooth. Season with salt and pepper.

For the tomato salsa:

½	large red onion, chopped
½	cup chopped fresh basil
1	pound ripe tomatoes, peeled, seeded and chopped
2	tablespoons grated Parmesan cheese
3	tablespoons fresh lime juice
2	tablespoons olive oil
1	tablespoon balsamic vinegar

Salt and black pepper

16	(½-inch) slices French baguette

Preheat the broiler. Combine the red onion, basil and tomatoes in a bowl. Mix in the cheese, lime juice, oil and vinegar. Season with salt and pepper. Set aside.

Spread the garlic butter on both sides of each slice of bread. Put the bread slices on a baking sheet. Broil until browned and crisp. Arrange the toasted bread on a platter, spoon salsa over each slice and serve.

Courtesy of Munson Farms

Edamame

Edamame (ed-a-MAH-may) are a variety of soybeans that are increasingly common at Colorado farmers' markets. They are nutrient-rich beans meant to be eaten in the green stage. You may sometimes hear them called sweet beans, green soybeans or vegetable soybeans. Though edamame have been cultivated in Asia since 200 B.C., they have only been grown in Colorado since 1998.

The peak season for edamame is from August until late September. You can use them in any recipe that calls for a cooked bean, such as soups, marinated salads and stir frys. They cook quickly, so add them at the end of the cooking time. I don't usually add them to recipes, because I like them just as they are – boiled and popped right from the pod. Raw edamame taste a bit like green peas, but they are typically cooked, giving them a mildly sweet taste.

The first time I ate edamame, I laboriously opened every pod and took out each separate bean – very tedious! The proper (and much simpler) way to eat the cooked beans is to hold the fuzzy pod and squeeze the beans out with your front teeth or fingers. It's amazing how fast you can go through a whole bowl this way.

Lauren Culbertson, of Pachamama Farms in Longmont, said that when she and her husband, Ewell, went to Japan to learn more about growing edamame, they were privileged to eat their meals in the farmers' homes. They were pleasantly surprised to see a bowl of cooked edamame set out at every single meal, including breakfast.

You can enjoy edamame year-round by purchasing the beans in summer and freezing them. Simply seal cooked beans in freezer bags and freeze. Follow the directions below for a delicious, healthy snack.

Cooked Edamame Beans

Always wash edamame extremely well before cooking – the fuzzy pods collect lots of dirt that needs to be completely removed.

For fresh beans, remove the pods from stems and rinse very well under cool water. Cook the pods in boiling, salted water for 4 to 7 minutes.

Cook frozen beans in boiling, salted water for 2 to 5 minutes, then drain them. Edamame can be served warm or cold. Refrigerate leftovers for a grab-and-go snack.

Article courtesy of Laura Korth, Longmont Farmers' Market

Fiorentinis

Chef Michael Angelo (Mick) Rosacci of Tony's Meats & Specialty Foods writes a weekly food and wine newspaper column, demonstrates seasonal cooking every week on Channel 7 news and teaches at Tony's Bowles Market Cooking School. His recipes reflect the seasons and use only the freshest ingredients. Fiorentinis are savory, flaky phyllo triangles stuffed with chopped steak, arugula and cheese. Bingham Hill Ghost Town is similar to a cheddar/parmesan. Harvest Moon is similar to a very sharp cheddar. You could substitute Bingham Hill Rustic Blue cheese, a dry Jack or a Canadian or Irish cheddar for the Bingham Hill cheeses.

Serves 4

8   ounces rib-eye steak (a leftover steak is ideal, or use ground sirloin)
Salt and black pepper
2   ounces fresh arugula, chopped
4-6 tablespoons grated Bingham Hill Ghost Town or Harvest Moon Cheese
1   tablespoon olive oil
1   package phyllo dough
Melted butter and/or olive oil for brushing (optional)

Season the steak with salt and pepper. Grill or fry the steak to rare or medium-rare. Cool and finely chop the steak. Combine the steak, arugula and grated cheese. Drizzle olive oil over the steak mixture and season with salt and pepper.

Preheat the oven to 400°F. Peel off 1 sheet of filo dough. Fold it in half and then into thirds to form a strip about 1½ to 2 inches wide. Brush one side of each strip with melted butter and/or olive oil. Place a spoonful of filling on one end and fold into a triangle (each sheet will make 1 to 2 appetizers). Bake on a baking sheet until browned, about 6 to 8 minutes.

Courtesy of Chef Mick Rosacci, Tony's Meats & Specialty Foods

Spring Vegetable Stack

Braddy's Downtown Restaurant in Fort Collins, exemplifies the modern Colorado Front Range style of cooking – a cuisine of place, that could best be called "Modern Western American." Their cooking is based upon quality, flavor and comfort. This recipe, like Braddy's, represents the best of Fort Collins: clean air, sunny days, beautiful scenery and a great quality of life. This dish goes well with a fresh baguette or rustic bread and a good, crisp white wine. Opal basil is a purple-hued basil available at many farmers' markets.

Serves 2

1   bunch asparagus
1   tablespoon extra virgin olive oil
Juice of ½ lemon
Salt and black pepper
1   English cucumber, peeled, halved lengthwise and seeded
1   tablespoon chopped fresh opal basil (or other fresh basil)
1   tablespoon chopped fresh tarragon
1   tablespoon chopped fresh chives
1   cup cooked couscous, tossed with a little extra virgin olive oil
1   large tomato, peeled, seeded and chopped
Balsamic vinegar

Trim the asparagus to ½-inch tops (if you can't get the skinny stuff, peel away the outside layers of the stalk). Blanch in boiling water until crisp-tender, about 2 minutes. Cool quickly in ice water, dry, then toss with the olive oil and lemon juice. Let stand at room temperature.

Chop the cucumber into a ¼-inch pieces. Put the basil, tarragon and chives in a small bowl and toss together. Place a 3-inch round ring mold in the center of a large plate. Pack half of the couscous tightly in the mold. Place half the cucumber on top and pack lightly. Add a light layer of herbs, reserving some for garnish. Place half of the chopped tomatoes in the mold next. Carefully remove the mold. Repeat the layers for the second plate. If you do not have a ring mold, line 2 small ramekins or custard cups with plastic wrap and pack the ingredients in reverse order – first the tomatoes, followed by herbs, cucumber and couscous. Invert on the plate and remove the plastic wrap.

Place the asparagus around the vegetable stack and garnish the plate with herbs. Drizzle the plate and stack with extra virgin olive oil and balsamic vinegar.

Courtesy of Braddy's Downtown Restaurant

CULTIVATE

NATURAL

USDA (top left); Paul Bousquet (middle left); Rich Abrahamson (top right); USDA (bottom)

Paul Bousquet

LOCAL FLAVOR

GARDEN

USDA (top left); Paul Bousquet (middle right); Colorado Fresh Markets/Cherry Creek Fresh Market (bottom)

EARLY
BIRD

RIPE

USDA (top right and bottom); Bob Castellino (middle left)

SALADS & DRESSINGS

Rocky Ford Melon

You have to be impressed when a farmer hands you a Rocky Ford melon and says, "Thank you, we'll see you at the next market." Is the farmer a fortune teller, or just that confident and proud? Either way, once you've tasted a luscious Rocky Ford cantaloupe, you will want to go back the next week, and the next.

Rocky Ford, a small farming community on the southeastern plains of Colorado, has what any melon farmer will tell you is the perfect soil for growing melons. It is no surprise that Rocky Ford has gained a national reputation for its superior melons.

Coloradans are proud of the melons that are grown in Rocky Ford and in other areas of the state, where conditions nurture juicy melons in all their varieties. Whether you want cantaloupe, honeydew or watermelon, finding good quality melon at the farmers' market is like trying to hit the broad side of a barn with a baseball – you can't miss. Nevertheless, there are some things to look for.

Cantaloupes should weigh two to four pounds and feel heavy and solid for their size. Also, look at the stem end. A ripe melon releases its stem, leaving a circular crevice that should be smooth and green, indicating that the melon was ready and its stem came away easily.

Of course, the perfume wafting through the air will tell you all you really need to know. Melons should be available into October, but are best earlier in the season because of the long days of sunshine. Store uncut cantaloupe at room temperature until serving. Once cut, cantaloupe should be stored airtight in the refrigerator, where it will last for several days. Let it come to room temperature before serving.

Rocky Ford Cantaloupe, Red Onion, Cucumber and Arugula Salad / Serves 4

This salad is a unique way to make use of fine quality melon. It makes a light lunch salad or an excellent side dish with spicy grilled shrimp.

½   Rocky Ford cantaloupe, cut in half
1   cucumber, peeled, seeded and sliced as thinly as possible
½   small red onion, thinly sliced
1   pound arugula, long stems removed
¼   cup pine nuts, toasted
Salt and black pepper
8   dashes green or red Tabasco
Juice of one lime
¼   cup extra virgin olive oil

Seed the melon and cut off the flesh. Chop the flesh into bite-size pieces. Put the melon, cucumber, onion, arugula and pine nuts in a bowl. Season liberally with salt and black pepper. Toss to combine. Mix the Tabasco and lime juice and sprinkle over the salad. Drizzle in enough olive oil to lightly coat. Toss again and serve.

Article and recipe courtesy of Sean Kelly, Claire de Lune

Fava Beans, Roasted Beets and Pecorino on Arugula

Jim Smailer of the Boulder Cork restaurant came from a family of cooks who encouraged his interest in food. His grandfather was his greatest influence. "He was a naturalist and he opened my eyes to lots of bits and pieces of nature that I apply in my cooking," Smailer explains. At the Cork, this inspiration is evident in the fresh and natural ingredients used to prepare each dish. This salad is a favorite of Smailer's. Fresh fava beans are available in late spring and fall, but can be difficult to find, even in season. Look for ones without beans bulging in the pods, which indicate that the beans are old and tough. If you cannot find fava beans, substitute fresh baby lima beans.

Serves 6

2   medium beets, washed
Olive oil
3   pounds fresh fava beans
½   pound arugula, washed and dried, tough stems removed
¼   pound Pecorino Romano cheese, sliced paper thin
1   teaspoon fresh lemon juice
½   cup extra virgin olive oil
1   tablespoon red wine vinegar
Salt and black pepper

Preheat the oven to 350°F. Brush the beets with a little olive oil and roast on a cookie sheet for 30 minutes, or until tender. Allow the beets to cool, then peel and cut into thin strips or chunks.

Remove the fava beans from the pods. Blanch the beans to help remove the tough skin. Arrange the arugula on 6 salad plates and top each with some beets, fava beans and Romano cheese.

Whisk together the lemon juice, olive oil and vinegar. Season with salt and pepper. Drizzle the dressing over each salad.

Adapted from a recipe courtesy of the Boulder Cork

Quinoa Salad

Quinoa (pronounced *keen-wah*) was a staple in the diet of the Inca and has been cultivated in the Andes of South America (and now in Colorado) for over 5,000 years. Quinoa is called "the super grain of the future" because of its high protein and low carbohydrate content. This salad may be served cold or at room temperature.

Serves 4

1	cup quinoa
1½	cups water
2	tomatoes, peeled, seeded and finely chopped
6	green onions, including tops, thinly sliced,
1	cup finely chopped parsley and/or cilantro
¼	cup chopped black olives

Lemon vinaigrette (recipe follows)

Rinse the quinoa until the water runs clear. Drain well and put in a medium saucepan. Add 1 cup of water. Bring to a boil, reduce the heat to low and cook, uncovered, for 15 to 20 minutes. Cool for 10 minutes, then add the tomatoes, onions, parsley and olives; toss with the lemon vinaigrette. Serve immediately.

For the lemon vinaigrette:

½	cup lemon or lime juice
2	tablespoons olive oil
½	teaspoon dried marjoram
½	teaspoon ground cumin

Black pepper

Whisk all of the ingredients together.

Courtesy of Green Earth Farms

Three Simple Salads with Raspberry Vinaigrette

Linda White and her husband started Longmont's Willow River Cheese Importers with only four varieties of cheese. "People weren't into cheese then like they are now," says White. "Many people didn't even know what Brie was." The Whites visited Boulder County restaurants giving away samples along with recipes to try. Their hard work began to pay off, as many local chefs switched to Willow River cheeses. At the same time, interest in sampling new cheeses increased nationwide. As the demand for different varieties grew, the Whites added new cheeses to their stock and today carry over 400 cheeses, from Appenzeller and Deux de Montagne to good old Monterey Jack.

Spinach Salad with Strawberries and Feta Cheese

Serves 6

12 ounces spinach, rinsed well, tough stems removed
1   cup strawberry halves
4   ounces Haystack Mountain Goat's Milk feta cheese, crumbled
¼   cup pistachios, shelled and toasted
Raspberry vinaigrette (recipe follows)

Put the spinach, strawberries, feta and pistachios in a large bowl. Use enough dressing to just moisten the spinach and toss. Add more dressing if desired. Serve immediately on chilled salad plates.

Pear, Gorgonzola and Walnut Salad

Serves 6

2   heads endive
3   Comice pears, peeled and sliced
6   ounces Gorgonzola cheese, crumbled
¼   cup chopped walnuts, toasted
Raspberry vinaigrette (recipe follows)

Arrange the endive leaves in a fan shape on chilled salad plates. Top with pears and sprinkle with Gorgonzola and walnuts. Drizzle with raspberry vinaigrette.

Spinach Salad with Tangerines and Pine Nuts

Serves 6

12 ounces spinach, rinsed well, tough stems removed
2 tangerines, peeled and sectioned
2 avocados, peeled and cut into large chunks
4 ounces Parmesan cheese, shaved with a cheese shaver or sharp knife
¼ cup pine nuts, toasted
Raspberry vinaigrette (recipe follows)

In a large bowl, toss the spinach with enough dressing to just moisten it. Divide the spinach among chilled salad plates. Top the spinach with tangerine sections, avocado chunks, a few shavings of Parmesan and a sprinkling of pine nuts. Drizzle a little more dressing over each salad and serve.

Raspberry Vinaigrette

This dressing goes well with the preceding cheese, fruit and nut salads.

Makes
2 cups

3 tablespoons raspberry vinegar
3 tablespoons fresh lemon juice
1 teaspoon Dijon mustard
1 clove garlic, minced
½ teaspoon salt
¼ teaspoon black pepper
¾ cup light olive oil
½ cup canola oil

Whisk the vinegar, lemon juice and mustard in a small bowl until the mustard is incorporated. Add the garlic, salt, pepper and oils, whisking constantly.

Courtesy of Willow River Cheese Importers

Arugula

Arugula's popularity has grown immensely over the last decade. It is now one of the most popular salad greens around. Its peppery, peanutty flavor – that is perhaps reminiscent of the radish – sets it apart from the more ordinary head lettuce.

Sometimes referred to as "rocket" or "ruchetta," Arugula is a member of the mustard family. It's deeply toothed leaves look strikingly similar to turnip tops. The leaves can be as small as two inches long, or as big as seven inches, though arugula is generally at its best somewhere in the middle. However, since its flavor becomes spicier as it gets bigger, baby arugula is preferable for those who prefer a milder flavor.

A general rule of thumb: the hotter the weather, the hotter the arugula, which makes it an ideal late spring or early fall salad green. Buy crisp arugula – arugula loses its flavor when it wilts. Besides its primary function as a salad star, it is also excellent in a light, simple pasta dish such as linguini with garlic and olive oil. Arugula can be stored for several days in airtight baggies in the refrigerator. Like any low growing green, arugula should be washed thoroughly just before serving.

Grilled Asparagus Salad with Arugula and Oven-Dried Tomatoes / Serves 6

9   Roma tomatoes, halved lengthwise
Olive oil and balsamic vinegar
¼   cup minced fresh herbs, such as thyme, basil, oregano, etc.
Salt and black pepper
Ice water
2   bunches asparagus, cut to equal lengths
½   pound arugula, stems removed and rinsed well
Balsamic vinaigrette (recipe follows)
6   large slices rustic-style bread
6   ounces blue cheese, crumbled

Preheat the oven to 275°F. Place the tomato halves on a cookie sheet cut-sides up. Sprinkle with olive oil, balsamic vinegar, fresh herbs and salt and pepper to taste. Bake the tomatoes for 2 hours. Remove the tomatoes from the oven and cool.

Fill a medium bowl with ice water and set aside. Fill a medium saucepan with water and add ½ teaspoon of salt. Bring to a boil. Place the asparagus in the boiling water and cook for 2 minutes. Drain the asparagus and immediately plunge into the ice water to stop the cooking and preserve its bright color. Drain and set aside.

Preheat the grill. Toss the arugula with just enough vinaigrette to coat the leaves. Divide it among 6 plates. Brush the asparagus and bread with a little olive oil. Season the asparagus with a little salt and pepper and grill it lightly, along with the bread slices.

Arrange the roasted tomatoes and grilled asparagus atop the greens on each plate. Top with cheese and drizzle a little vinaigrette around the plate. Set the grilled bread on the side of the plate and serve.

For the balsamic vinaigrette:
½   cup balsamic vinegar
1   cup olive oil
1   teaspoon minced shallot
½   teaspoon minced garlic
Salt and black pepper

Whisk all of the ingredients together.

Article and recipe courtesy of Sean Kelly, Claire de Lune

Baked Goat Cheese and Field Green Salad

This salad features fresh field greens with Mediterranean accents. It is topped with rounds of warm, bread crumb-coated goat cheese. For the field greens, try a mixture of arugula, radicchio, mache, baby red oak, frisée, baby romaine, Belgian endive, etc. Your farmers' market or grocery should have a pre-made mix of field greens that would be perfect.

Serves 4

1 pound assorted mixed greens, washed and dried
Balsamic vinaigrette (recipe follows)
1 11-ounce log goat cheese
2 tablespoons olive oil
1 cup dried bread crumbs
2 tablespoons pine nuts, toasted
12 Niçoise olives, or other black olives
½ cup peeled and chopped tomato

Preheat the oven to 500°F. Toss the field greens with the balsamic vinaigrette. Just before you plate the salad, prepare the cheese.

Slice the goat cheese into 8 disk-shaped pieces. Brush each disk lightly with olive oil and dip in the bread crumbs to coat evenly. Bake for 2 minutes, or until the cheese is lightly browned and heated through (be careful not to overcook the cheese – the goal is to warm the cheese, not melt it).

Divide the salad greens among 4 plates and sprinkle each with toasted pine nuts. Garnish with olives and tomatoes. Top each salad with warm goat cheese and serve immediately.

For the balsamic vinaigrette:
1 teaspoon minced shallots
1 teaspoon minced garlic
1 tablespoon Dijon mustard
2 tablespoons balsamic vinegar
¾ cup extra virgin olive oil
1 teaspoon fresh lemon or lime juice
Kosher salt and freshly ground black pepper

Whisk together the shallots, garlic, mustard and vinegar. Slowly whisk in the olive oil so that the dressing emulsifies (does not separate). Whisk in the lemon or lime juice and season with salt and pepper.

Courtesy of Cuisine Catering

Nine-Day Slaw

The Front Range Organic Gardeners club is dedicated to education and out-reach on organic gardening and environmental issues. This slaw highlights many locally grown products. Unlike slaws made with mayonnaise, this vinegar-based version easily lasts nine days in the refrigerator. It is a very colorful mixture combining sweet and sour flavors, that is a healthy addition to a summer barbecue. Note: the slaw needs to refrigerated overnight.

Serves
8 to 10

1½ pounds cabbage, shredded
½   green bell pepper, chopped
½   red bell pepper, chopped
1   small onion, chopped
3   carrots, peeled and sliced (or shredded)
½   cup sugar

In a large bowl, combine the cabbage, green and red bell peppers onion and carrots. Stir in the sugar and blend well. Set the vegetables aside while you make the dressing.

For the slaw dressing:
½   cup distilled white vinegar
½   cup canola oil
½   teaspoon salt
1   tablespoon sugar
1   tablespoon celery seed
½-1 teaspoon yellow mustard
Tabasco to taste (optional)

In a small sauce pan, blend together all of the dressing ingredients. Bring the mixture to a boil in a small saucepan. Immediately pour the boiling dressing over the cabbage and mix thoroughly. Let cool, then cover and store in the refrigerator overnight before serving.

Courtesy of Front Range Organic Gardeners

Grandma's Potato Salad

McCurry Farms has been bringing quality produce to farmers' markets for over 30 years. The farm raises Rocky Ford cantaloupes, watermelon, sweet corn, green chiles, pumpkins and summer and winter squash. This potato salad may well replace your old family recipe. It has a tangy flavor and the unpeeled cucumber and red pepper add a lovely element of color. Make sure the eggs and potatoes have cooled before mixing them with the other ingredients.

Serves 8 to 10

5	red potatoes, peeled
3	hard boiled eggs, cooled, peeled and finely chopped
1	unpeeled cucumber, coarsely grated or finely chopped
1	medium yellow onion, finely chopped
1	large stalk celery, finely chopped
1	4-ounce jar chopped pimentos (or ½ cup chopped, roasted red bell pepper)
1	cup mayonnaise
1	teaspoon salt
1	teaspoon black pepper
1	teaspoon sugar

Distilled white vinegar to taste

Boil the potatoes until tender. Cool the potatoes and then finely chop them. Put the potatoes and eggs in a large bowl. Add the cucumber, onion, celery and pimentos; mix well.

To make the dressing, combine the mayonnaise, salt, pepper and sugar in a bowl and stir well. Add vinegar to taste. Add the dressing to the potato mixture and gently toss to combine. Garnish with paprika and parsley. Refrigerate until serving.

Courtesy of McCurry Farms

Authentic German Potato Salad

Gwin Farms is a small family farm that produces hay, natural, corn-fed beef, eggs and a small quantity of vegetables, all grown without chemicals or pesticides. The Gwins have been selling at the Longmont Farmers' Market since 1994. Judy Gwin's German grandmother, Mary, who lived to be 104, taught her this recipe – only the original recipe called for "a handful" of this and "a pinch" of that. This salad can be served as a side dish, and goes well with poultry, pork and other meats. It is served hot and is comforting on dreary winter days.

Serves
4 to 6

5-6	medium Colorado red or Yukon Gold potatoes, peeled
8	strips bacon, chopped into ½-inch pieces
¾	cup chopped white onion
2	heaping tablespoons flour
⅓	cup cider vinegar
⅔	cup water

Boil the potatoes in salted water until tender. Drain and cool the potatoes, then coarsely chop them and set aside.

Cook the bacon until crisp; drain on paper towels, reserving the bacon drippings. In the same pan used to cook the bacon, cook the onions with 1 tablespoon of the reserved bacon drippings over medium heat until the onions are translucent. Sprinkle the flour over the onions and stir to blend. Continue cooking for a few minutes, stirring constantly, and being careful not to burn the flour.

Add the vinegar and water and bring to a boil, stirring constantly with a whisk. Reduce the heat and simmer until thickened, whisking occasionally. Add the bacon, stir and then immediately pour the mixture over the potatoes. Toss well to blend. Serve hot.

Courtesy of Gwin Farm

Baked Goat Cheese and Baby Lettuce with Orange Vinaigrette

Boulder County's award-winning Haystack Goat Dairy uses a variety of goats to produce its delicious cheeses, primarily Nubian and Saanen, plus a small herd of Cashmere and Angora goats. The exotic looking Nubians have Roman noses and long floppy ears. The Saanens are an old Swiss breed. The mix of milk from these goats produces delicious, high-quality cheeses. This recipe is from Jason McHugh of Cooking School of the Rockies. The salad should be prepared and "plated" just before the cheese comes out of the oven, so it can be served immediately. A tip for using honey is to warm it first. This makes it easier to measure and to mix with other ingredients.

Serves 4

¼	cup olive oil
8	rounds Haystack Mountain goat cheese
2	teaspoons chopped fresh thyme
2	teaspoons chopped fresh tarragon
2	teaspoons chopped fresh rosemary
1	tablespoon chopped fresh parsley

Freshly ground black pepper
¾   pound baby lettuce, washed and dried
4   tablespoons roughly chopped hazelnuts, toasted
Orange vinaigrette (recipe follows)
Orange sections (optional)

Preheat the oven to 350°F. Put the oil in a small bowl and the herbs in a second small bowl. Dip each cheese round in the oil, then toss the rounds with the herbs to coat. Put the goat cheese on a baking sheet and season with pepper. Bake the cheese for 5 minutes, or until warmed through , but not melting.

While the cheese bakes, prepare the salads. In a large bowl, toss the lettuce with the vinaigrette just to coat. Arrange the salad on individual plates and garnish with the hazelnuts and orange sections. Place 2 baked goat cheese rounds atop each salad and serve immediately.

For the orange vinaigrette:
½   cup freshly squeezed orange juice
1   small shallot, peeled and minced
1   tablespoon honey
2   tablespoons champagne vinegar
½   cup canola oil
1   teaspoon orange oil or orange extract
Salt and white pepper

Put the orange juice and shallots in a small saucepan and bring to a boil. Reduce the juice to 2 tablespoons, then, off the heat, add the honey and stir until it is dissolved into the juice. Cool the mixture.

When the orange juice mixture is cooled, combine it with the vinegar and season with salt. Taste the combination and add more vinegar if desired. Whisk in the canola oil or combine everything in a blender. Add the orange oil and correct the seasoning with salt and white pepper.

Courtesy of Haystack Mountain Goat Dairy

Rustic Blue Cheese Salad Dressing

Tom and Kristi Johnson made the first batch of their unique, award-winning Bingham Hill Rustic Blue Cheese in 1999. It is the star of this easy blue cheese dressing, which tastes great on greens, especially spinach. Try sprinkling blue cheese crumbles on cooked beet greens or steamed beets. Sprinkle large chunks of Rustic Blue and some fresh or dried fruit and/or roasted walnuts on your salad, or experiment by adding small bits of fresh herbs to the dressing. The cheese is salty, so don't add any salt until you've tasted the finished dressing.

Makes
1 cup

½   cup olive oil
1   tablespoon white wine vinegar
2   tablespoons lemon juice
¼   cup crumbled Bingham Hill Rustic Blue Cheese, or other blue cheese
Dash of dry mustard
Dash of paprika
Black pepper

Place all of the ingredients in a pint jar with a lid (or similar container). Shake well to break up the cheese. Experiment by adding small bits of fresh herbs. Refrigerate any unused dressing.

Courtesy of Bingham Hill Cheese Company

Chicken and Almond Waldorf Salad with Dijon Dressing

Ben Davis, executive chef at Tony's Meats & Specialty Foods in Littleton, has been teaching a Farmers' Market class at the Seasoned Chef Cooking School in Denver since 2000 (after originally doing the class at the San Francisco Embarcadero Farmers' Market in the 1990's).

Serves 4

1	teaspoon paprika
½	teaspoon dried tarragon
2	teaspoons kosher salt
½	teaspoon freshly ground black pepper
1	tablespoon olive oil
2	boneless, skinless chicken breasts, halved
2	Granny Smith apples, peeled, cored and cut into 1-inch chunks
2	cups halved red or green seedless grapes
1	cup sliced celery
¼	cup crumbled blue cheese

Juice of ½ lemon

½	cup blanched, slivered almonds
2	tablespoons mayonnaise
2	teaspoons Dijon mustard
1	tablespoon apple cider vinegar
½	teaspoon brown sugar
1	head Belgian endive

Preheat the oven to 350°F. Combine the paprika, tarragon, salt, black pepper and olive oil in a small bowl and stir to mix. Add the chicken breasts and turn to coat. Wrap the chicken breasts in foil and bake for 20 minutes. Remove from the oven and cool to room temperature.

Combine the apples, grapes, celery, blue cheese and lemon juice. Set aside. Toast the almonds in a skillet until golden brown. Set aside.

Make the dressing by combining the mayonnaise, mustard, vinegar and brown sugar. Season with salt and pepper. Combine the dressing with the apple mixture.

Separate the leaves of the endive and arrange on plates or in a bowl. Top with the apple mixture. Slice the chicken breasts lengthwise and arrange over the top of the salad. Garnish with the toasted almonds and serve.

Courtesy of Chef Ben Davis, Tony's Meats & Specialty Foods

Cucumbers

When you consider the phrase "cool as a cucumber," it is easy to see how it makes sense. The cucumber, which originated in India and Egypt, is a member of the gourd family and is 96 percent water. Cucumbers were often carried by desert caravans because their green skin so effectively contains the cool, liquid-rich flesh within.

Cucumber season starts in the heat of the summer. And while our caravans now have air conditioning, the crisp, refreshing qualities of the cucumber are never more appreciated than during the scorching days of July and August. Nothing lowers your thermostat better than a cool cucumber salad or a bowl of gazpacho.

There are several different types of cucumbers, but probably only three that you will encounter at the farmers' market. The first to arrive at the market is the Kirby, a small, bumpy and usually slightly curved variety that is used for pickling. A second type is the longer, dark green variety with which most of us are familiar, and the farmers simply call "slicers." The third type is the English cucumber, which are typically wrapped in plastic because their skin is so thin that they would dry out otherwise. English cucumbers are considered seedless because their seeds are so small.

Don't be misled if you find farmers' market cucumbers to be less shiny than the grocery store variety – this is a good thing – grocery store cucumbers are usually coated with wax to increase their shelf life. Any of the varieties need only feel firm and heavy for their size and be free of cuts or blemishes. Avoid very large cucumbers, though, as their flesh shrinks to make way for larger, firmer seeds.

Kirbies, because of their rough surface, should be scrubbed with a soft vegetable brush before using. Whether or not to peel a cucumber is a matter of personal preference, unless it has been in your refrigerator too long (the skin turns bitter with age). This shouldn't be a problem for cucumbers bought fresh. Cucumbers will last for one to two weeks in a plastic bag in the refrigerator, but like all fresh produce, once it's picked, it loses a little flavor every day.

Cucumber, Goat Cheese & Mint Salad with Olives / Serves 4 to 6

This salad offers a fantastic blend of Mediterranean flavors. Try making it with Haystack Mountain's delicious and mild fresh goat's milk feta cheese. The salad is good served at room temperature, or slightly chilled for hot days.

3   cucumbers, peeled, seeded and sliced in half-moon shapes
½   red onion, thinly sliced
1½   tablespoons chopped fresh mint leaves
2-3 tablespoons red wine vinegar
4-6 tablespoons extra virgin olive oil
15   oil-cured black olives, pitted
4   ounces crumbled goat cheese, feta or ricotta salata
Salt and black pepper

Put the cucumbers, red onion, mint, vinegar and olive oil in a stainless steel bowl. Toss to combine. Allow the salad to stand at room temperature for about 30 minutes. Before serving, add the olives and cheese. Toss gently. Season with salt and pepper.

Article and recipe courtesy of Sean Kelly, Claire de Lune

The Perfect Vinaigrette

Chet Anderson of The Fresh Herb Company says, "A really good vinaigrette is one thing people struggle to make. The key is to use the best products you can find – extra virgin olive oil and the best balsamic vinegar." The following recipe is made with a three to one ratio of oil to vinegar. For a less sharp-tasting dressing, use four parts oil to one part vinegar. Using this recipe as a base, experiment a little. For raspberry vinaigrette, crush overripe raspberries and strain the juice into the basic vinaigrette. Toasted pine nuts or other nuts are delicious with the vinaigrette. Also good are roasted red peppers or different cheeses. Or, use the dressing to make a Greek salad by combining salad greens with feta cheese, kalamata olives, cucumber, dried oregano, tomatoes and red onion.

Makes
2 cups

4	shallots, minced
1	teaspoon salt
½	cup balsamic vinegar
1½	cups extra virgin olive oil

In a bowl or jar, combine the shallots, salt and vinegar; stir the mixture until the salt has dissolved. Gradually add the oil, whisking constantly. Adjust the flavors to your taste.

Courtesy of The Fresh Herb Company

Steak and Roasted Vegetable Salad

This is a surprisingly easy and light entrée salad of lean beef, mixed greens and roasted vegetables.

Serves 4

1	medium zucchini, cut diagonally into 1-inch dice
1	medium Japanese or baby eggplant, peeled and cut in diagonal 1-inch dice
1	large red, yellow or green bell pepper, cut into 1-inch strips
1	medium onion, cut into 1-inch slices
16	small white mushrooms

Olive oil-flavored cooking spray

2	tablespoons balsamic vinegar
2	large cloves garlic, crushed
1	teaspoon dried rosemary leaves, crushed
¼	teaspoon black pepper
1	pound 1-inch thick boneless top loin steaks

Salt

8	cups torn mixed salad greens
¾	cup Perfect Vinaigrette (page 56) or Balsamic Vinaigrette (page 42)

Preheat the oven to 425°F. Lightly spray a 10x15-inch jellyroll pan or baking sheet with cooking spray. Place the vegetables in the pan and generously spray with cooking spray. Or, place the vegetables in a plastic bag with 2 tablespoons of olive oil and shake to coat.

Combine the vinegar, garlic, rosemary and pepper drizzle over the vegetables. Marinate the vegetables for 10 to 20 minutes, then roast the vegetables for 30 to 35 minutes, until tender, stirring once halfway through the cooking time.

Meanwhile, heat a large, non-stick skillet over medium heat. Add the steaks and cook for 12 to 15 minutes for medium-rare to medium doneness, turning once halfway through the cooking time. Remove the steaks from the heat and let rest for 10 minutes. Trim any fat and carve cross-wise into thin slices. Season lightly with salt.

To serve, divide the salad greens among 4 plates. Arrange the steak slices and roasted vegetables over the greens. Serve immediately with Perfect Vinaigrette or Balsamic Vinaigrette.

Courtesy of Colorado Beef Council

Marinated Cucumbers

This cool, crisp cucumber salad offers a nice balance of salty and sweet – perfect for hot summer days. The salt helps take away any bitterness in the cucumber.

Serves 4

2   cucumbers, peeled and halved lengthwise
1   teaspoon salt
¼   cup cider vinegar
¼   cup water
3   tablespoons sugar
Fresh dill weed to garnish

Scrape the seeds from the inside of the cucumber halves and thinly slice them. Put the slices in a colander and sprinkle them with salt. Let sit for 15 minutes.

Combine the vinegar, water and sugar in a medium bowl. Stir until the sugar has dissolved. Rinse the cucumber slices under cold running water and drain well. Add the cucumbers to the vinegar mixture and refrigerate for at least 15 minutes. Sprinkle with dill before serving.

Courtesy of Pueblo Farmers Marketeers

SOUPS

Cream of Zucchini Soup with Fresh Basil

Use up some of your bounty of end-of-the-season zucchini in this flavorful soup. It is surprisingly light – don't let the cream frighten you away. It can be served as a first course, or with a salad and some bread as a light supper. The garnish of sour cream and fresh basil provides a colorful contrast atop the green and cream colored soup. You can also chop up a few basil leaves and stir them into the soup for added flavor.

Serves 6

2	tablespoons butter
½	cup chopped green onion, including the green tops
2	pounds zucchini (about 5 medium), sliced
3	cups chicken or vegetable broth
½	cup packed fresh basil leaves
1½	cups half & half

Pinch of white pepper
Salt

½	cup sour cream or plain yogurt
6	sprigs fresh basil

Melt the butter in a 4-quart saucepan over medium heat. Add the green onion and cook for 5 minutes, stirring occasionally, until the onions are soft. Add the zucchini and cook for 3 minutes more, stirring occasionally.

Add the chicken broth and bring to a boil over high heat. Reduce the heat and simmer, uncovered, for 20 minutes. Add the basil and mix well. Allow the soup to cool slightly.

Purée the soup in a blender or food processor, then return the mixture to the saucepan. Stir in the half & half, white pepper and salt. Reheat and serve hot, or chill the soup and serve it cold (if you serve the soup cold, check the seasoning – it may need more salt). Serve garnished with a dollop of sour cream or plain yogurt and a sprig of basil.

Courtesy of Munson Farms

Raspberry Riesling Soup with Cantaloupe Sorbet

This soup is slightly sweet and slightly tart – just the right balance. It makes a dramatic presentation served in cantaloupe shells with cantaloupe sorbet. Try making the soup using Plum Creek Cellars' Riesling Ice Wine from Palisade.

Serves 8

1	cup sugar
¾	cup water
¾	cup fresh lemon juice
4	small cantaloupes, halved and hollowed out enough to hold 1 cup of soup, reserving 2 cups of the flesh
2	cups fresh raspberries
4	cups Riesling, or other slightly sweet white wine

Refrigerate the cantaloupe shell until ready to use. Put the sugar, water and lemon juice in a small saucepan over medium heat. Stir until the sugar dissolves, then heat the mixture until it comes just to the boiling point. Remove from the heat and set aside.

Chop the reserved canteloupe flesh, then purée it until smooth. Strain the purée through a mesh strainer into a medium bowl. "Season" the purée with 1 cup of the lemon syrup, more or less to taste, depending on the sweetness of the melon (The mixture should taste slightly sweeter than you would like, because once it is frozen, it will taste less sweet).

Freeze the puréed mixture in an ice cream machine, or pour it into a loaf pan and freeze until solid. Remove from the freezer and let thaw slightly. Break into large chunks and place in a bowl. Beat until well-blended but still frozen. Return the mixture to the loaf pan, cover and freeze solid.

Meanwhile, in a food processor or blender, purée the raspberries with the wine. Strain the mixture through a mesh strainer into a bowl to remove the raspberry seeds. Add enough lemon syrup to yield a mildly sweet, yet tart soup. Chill the soup, then adjust the "seasoning" with more lemon syrup if needed. Ladle the soup into the cantaloupe bowls and serve with the cantaloupe sorbet.

Courtesy of Cook Street School of Fine Cooking

Sweet Corn

In July, the competition is fierce among the farmers to see who will be the first to bring sweet corn to the farmers' markets. Farmers plant corn in succession and then pick each new patch as it matures so, no matter when in the season you buy their corn, you're getting a fresh ear that tastes wonderful.

There are many varieties of corn available at the markets, most of which fall into one of three categories: yellow, bi-color and white. The differences among the three varities are found in the size of the kernels, the number of rows per ear and the dates of maturity. Happily, long-lasting sweetness is a feature shared by all three.

Corn growers face many obstacles to a full harvest – drought, hailstorms, wind and the dreaded raccoon. These furry little creatures with the cute face and finger-like claws can decimate an entire corn field in a single night. They love corn, but, like judges at the county fair, they only sample. They take one or two bites from every ear – just enough to render it unfit for sale – and eat their way down each row in the field. Raccoons are smart, too. They always seem to be one step ahead of the farmer in knowing the moment when each patch has reached the perfect ripeness, and they plan their evening raids accordingly. They commonly dismantle the plastic irrigation pipes to fill an area with water for a cool drink after their feast. One farmer commented that when there are dozens of raccoons in the field, it sounds like machinery at work.

Obstacles aside, we are very fortunate in the amount and quality of corn that we have in Colorado. Local farmers plant varieties that will provide optimum taste and tenderness, not those that are bred to withstand the shipping process. Gone are the days of passing up the larger ears, thinking them to be old and tough. Some new varieties simply have more rows of kernels per ear – 18 to 22 rows instead of the standard 14, thus producing larger ears of the same high quality.

If you can't fight the urge to strip down the ear and inspect it before purchasing, you may want to try this method instead: simply move down to the middle of the ear and gently ease back the husk with your thumb. This way you get a "peek" at the corn and see if it's what you're looking for. Then move the husk back into place. Thus, if you decide not to buy it, it is still in good shape for other customers.

Taking my cue from hungry farmers at the market, I have learned that raw corn is absolutely wonderful. It's cool, sweet, crisp and nutritious – the perfect treat. If you

haven't tried grilled corn on the cob, use this easy method the next time you're barbecuing: Pull back the husks just enough to remove the silk. Replace the husks and tie the top with a strip of husk, like a pale green ribbon. Soak the corn in water for one minute. This will allow the corn to steam a little as it grills. Grill the corn, turning once or twice during the cooking time, usually four to five minutes.

Summer Corn Chowder / Serves 4

For recipes calling for corn off the cob, such as this chowder, husk the corn and remove the silk with a tea towel. Hold the cob vertically over a bowl or platter, tilt slightly and cut down the cob to remove just the top two-thirds of the kernels, then rotate the cob for a new set of rows. After all the kernels have been removed, turn the knife around and, using the dull back edge, scrape downward to extract as much "milk" from the cob as possible.

1	stick butter
1	medium onion, chopped
1	large leek, or 2 bunches green onions, thinly sliced
2	cloves garlic, minced
4-5	new potatoes, chopped into small chunks
6	ears sweet corn, kernels cut off, cobs milked (one cob reserved)
½	teaspoon seeded and minced jalapeño (optional)
1½	cups milk
1½	cups chicken broth, vegetable broth or water
¼	cup strips fresh basil
¼	teaspoon salt

Melt the butter over medium-low heat. Add the onion and leeks; cook until soft, but not browned. Add the garlic and cook for 1 more minute. Add the potatoes, corn, corn "milk" and jalapeño. Cook for 10 minutes, stirring every minute or so. Add the milk, broth and reserved corn cob. Bring to a low boil, reduce the heat and simmer until the potatoes and corn are completely soft and the soup is slightly thickened. Remove the corn cob and serve.

Article courtesy of Laura Korth, Longmont Farmers' Market; Recipe courtesy of Sean Kelly, Claire de Lune

Tortilla Soup

Chef Michael Hanrahan, of the Vail Valley's Cuisine Catering, has won more "People's Choice" awards than any other mountain chef. This amazing tortilla soup is a good example of Hanrahan's talent. As it is written, the recipe is very mild – just add more jalapeño if you want it spicier. For a chunkier soup, skip the puréeing. For an exceptional table-side presentation, fill soup bowls with the chicken, avocado and tortilla strips and place them on the table. Then ladle the steaming broth into each bowl "tableside."

Serves 6

1	tablespoon vegetable oil
8	6-inch corn tortillas, chopped into 1-inch pieces
1	cup chopped onion
1½	tablespoons seeded and minced jalapeño
5	cloves garlic, minced
1	tablespoon tomato paste
3	14.5-ounce cans whole tomatoes, undrained
1	tablespoon ground cumin
6	10.5-ounce cans low-salt chicken broth
2	cups shredded cooked boneless, skinless chicken breast (about 1 pound)
1	cup chopped avocado
½	cup shredded sharp cheddar cheese
½	cup chopped fresh cilantro

Heat the oil in a large ovenproof casserole dish or saucepan over medium-high heat. Add half the tortilla pieces and cook for 2 minutes, stirring occasionally, until crisp. Add the onion, jalapeño and garlic. Cook for 3 minutes. Add the tomato paste, tomatoes and tomato liquid, stirring until the tomato paste is mixed in. Bring to a simmer and cook for 10 minutes. Stir in the cumin and chicken broth. Bring to a boil, reduce the heat and simmer, uncovered, for 40 minutes, or until the soup is reduced to 8 cups. Let the soup cool a little.

Preheat the oven to 400°F. Purée half of the soup in a blender or food processor. Return the puréed soup to the pan and heat thoroughly over medium-high heat.

Arrange the remaining tortilla strips in a single layer on a baking sheet and bake for 7 minutes, or until crisp. Set aside.

Divide the chicken and avocado among 6 soup bowls, then pour soup into the bowls and serve immediately, or serve it tableside as described above. Top with cheddar cheese, cilantro and additional toasted tortilla strips.

Courtesy of Cuisine Catering

Fall Vegetable and Beef Soup

This soup is a perfect example of comfort food – it is thick and flavorful, just the thing to warm you up on a cold day. And, it is rich in vitamins A and C, calcium and iron. You can freeze any leftovers without diminishing the flavor.

Serves 8

1	pound Coleman Natural lean ground beef
1	medium onion, chopped
1	green bell pepper, seeded and chopped
2	tablespoons chili powder
½	teaspoon salt
2	cloves garlic, minced
1	28-ounce can whole tomatoes, undrained
5	medium potatoes, peeled and chopped into ½-inch cubes
4	medium carrots, peeled and thinly sliced
2	beef bouillon cubes, crushed
6	cups water
1	bay leaf
¼	teaspoon black pepper
½	small head cabbage, coarsely shredded (about 4 cups)

Grated Parmesan cheese to garnish

Spray the insides of a soup pot with cooking spray. Crumble the beef into the pot and cook over medium-high heat, stirring until the pink color is gone. Add the onion, bell pepper, chili powder and salt. Continue to cook for 8 to 10 minutes, stirring often, until the onion is lightly browned.

Mix in the garlic. Add the tomatoes (breaking them up into smaller pieces) and tomato liquid, potatoes, carrots and bouillon. Stir until the bouillon cubes have dissolved. Stir in the water, bay leaf and pepper.

Bring the mixture to a boil, reduce the heat, cover and simmer for 1 hour. (At this point you can cool, cover and refrigerate until the next day. Skim any fat before reheating.)

Stir in the cabbage. Increase the heat to medium and cook for 10 to 15 minutes, uncovered, just until the cabbage is tender but still bright green. Skim and discard any surface fat, if necessary. Season to taste with salt. Divide the soup among warm soup bowls. Pass Parmesan cheese to garnish.

Courtesy of Coleman Natural Products

Frantic French Onion Soup

The Muratas have been farming for three generations, growing onions, pinto beans, barley, wheat and feed corn. This recipe yields restaurant-quality French onion soup in 10 minutes. The secret is to make the Easy Caramelized Onions ahead of time.

Serves 4

2	14-ounce cans beef or vegetable broth
1	14-ounce can fat-free chicken or vegetable broth
¼	cup dry sherry
1	tablespoon Worcestershire sauce
½	teaspoon minced garlic
¼	teaspoon dried thyme
2	cups Easy Caramelized Onions (recipe follows)
4	ounces sliced Swiss cheese
2	cups plain or garlic-flavored croutons, or sliced day-old baguette, toasted
¼	cup grated Parmesan cheese, plus more to taste

Place a broiler rack 6-inches from the heat and preheat the broiler. Combine the beef and chicken broth (or vegetable broth), sherry, Worcestershire, garlic and thyme in a large soup pot or Dutch oven over high heat. Stir well and cover. When the broth comes to a boil, add the caramelized onions, stir well and cover. Return to a boil, reduce the heat to medium and cook until the soup is very hot.

Divide the soup among 4 oven-proof bowls. Sprinkle each bowl with ½ cup of croutons or cover with baguette slices. Lay a slice of Swiss cheese on top. Sprinkle each cheese slice with 1 tablespoon Parmesan cheese, or more to taste.

Place the bowls of soup on a baking sheet under the broiler for 1 minute, or until the cheese melts. Using pot holders, remove from the oven and serve at once. (Warn your guests that the bowls are very hot!) Serve with more Parmesan cheese.

For the easy caramelized onions:

This recipe produces beautiful brown onions, so full of flavor that all they need is a bit of broth, a splash of sherry and some cheese for Frantic French Onion Soup. Use leftover caramelized onions to top grilled steak, pork chops or chicken, or stir them into a casserole or stew. The onions may be airtight in the refrigerator for up to 3 days, or frozen for up to 1 month.

6	large onions, cut into ¼-inch slices
2	tablespoons olive oil
½	teaspoon salt
¼	teaspoon sugar

Put the onions in a slow cooker, drizzle with the oil and sprinkle with salt and sugar; stir to mix well. Place the lid on the cooker and turn it to high. Cook for 8 to 10 hours, until the onions caramelize – they will have a deep brown color.

If you do not have a slow-cooker, you can caramelize onions in a large skillet. Melt 4 tablespoons of butter (or 2 tablespoons butter and 2 tablespoons olive oil). Add the sliced onions and sprinkle with the salt and sugar; stir to mix well. Cover and cook over low heat for 30 to 45 minutes, stirring occasionally, until the onions are very soft. Raise the heat to medium and cook, stirring constantly, until the onions are browned, being careful not to burn them. Remove the onions and deglaze the pan by adding 2 tablespoons of white wine or broth and scraping the bottom of the pan. Stir this mixture into the onions and they are ready to use.

Courtesy of Murata Farms

Quinoa Soup

This soup may be very nutritious, but don't hold that against it. It tastes great and is easy to prepare.

Serves 4

1	tablespoon olive oil
1	red onion, chopped
1	celery stalk, chopped
1	cup cooked black beans, or 1 cup canned
1	medium potato, peeled and chopped
1	carrot, peeled and chopped
½	cup chopped parsley
1	clove garlic, minced
6	cups chicken or vegetable broth
½	cup vegetable juice cocktail (such as V-8 juice)
½	cup quinoa

Croutons for garnish
Shredded cheese for garnish

Heat the oil in a large saucepan over medium heat. Add the onion, celery, potato, black beans and carrot. Cook for 5 minutes. Stir in the parsley and garlic and cook for 1 more minute. Add the broth and vegetable juice and bring to a boil. Add the quinoa and return to a boil. Cover, reduce heat and simmer for 45 minutes, until the quinoa is cooked. Garnish with croutons and/or cheese.

Courtesy of Green Earth Farms

Black Bean Soup with Cilantro Cream

This is a wonderful alternative to winter-time chili. If you prefer a chunkier soup or whole beans, purée only part of the soup, or omit the puréeing all together.

Serves
4 to 6

½	cup sun-dried tomato halves (not oil-packed)
1	cup boiling water
4	slices bacon, chopped
1	small onion, chopped
1	15-ounce can black beans, rinsed and drained
1	14-ounce can chicken broth
1	clove garlic, minced
½	teaspoon ground cumin
¼	teaspoon hot pepper sauce
½	teaspoon ground coriander
1½	tablespoons lime juice
¼	cup chopped fresh cilantro

Cilantro cream (recipe follows)

Combine the dried tomatoes and boiling water. Let stand until the tomatoes are softened, about 30 minutes. Drain, reserving the liquid. Chop the tomatoes and set aside.

In a large saucepan, cook the bacon and onion over medium heat until the onions are soft. Drain off the fat. Add the tomatoes, reserved tomato soaking liquid, beans, broth, garlic, cumin, hot pepper sauce, coriander and lime juice; mix well. Bring to a boil over high heat. Lower the heat, cover and simmer for 5 minutes. Remove from the heat and stir in the cilantro. Let the soup cool slightly.

In a blender or food processor, purée the soup in batches. Put the puréed soup in a large saucepan and heat until it begins to boil. Ladle the soup into warm bowls, drizzle with the cilantro cream and serve immediately.

For the cilantro cream:

¼	cup sour cream or plain yogurt
1	tablespoon minced fresh cilantro
½	teaspoon ground coriander
1½	tablespoons lime juice

Combine all of the ingredients in a small bowl and mix well.

Courtesy of Kelley Bean

MOUTH WATERING

SUNRISE

Mark Fox (top left); Bob Castellino (top right); Rich Abrahamson (bottom)

VINE RIPENED

CULTIVATE

Bob Castellino (top left); Colorado Fresh Markets/Cherry Creek Fresh Market (top right); Mark Fox (bottom)

Paul Bousquet

JUICY

FESTIVALS

USDA (top right); Rich Abrahamson (middle left); USDA (middle right); Mark Fox (bottom)

Sweet Potato Soup with Sour Cream and Jalapeño

This is a very creamy soup with a surprising combination of flavors. The jalapeño adds just the right kick.

Serves 6 to 8

2   tablespoons bacon fat, butter or vegetable oil
1   pound red onions, chopped
1   leek, trimmed and chopped
1   jalapeño, seeded and minced (or add more for a spicier soup)
2   cloves garlic, minced
1½   pounds sweet potatoes, peeled and cut into ½-inch cubes
8   cups chicken broth
¼   teaspoon thyme
¼   teaspoon nutmeg
1   cup heavy cream or half & half
Salt and white pepper
Sour cream, to garnish

In a stock pot, heat the fat over medium heat. Add the onions, leeks and jalapeño; cook until the onions are soft. Add the garlic and cook for 1 more minute. Add the potatoes, broth, thyme and nutmeg. Bring the mixture to a boil, reduce the heat and simmer until the potatoes are soft. Cool the soup slightly, then purée it in batches. Return the puréed soup to the pot. Add the cream and mix well. Reheat the soup, then season to taste with salt and white pepper. Garnish with a dollop of sour cream and serve.

Courtesy of Cuisine Catering

Chilled Strawberry Soup with Chardonnay Vanilla Sauce

This soup, from Denver's Fourth Story restaurant, can be served as a starter, a dessert or as something to refresh your palate between courses. It uses an original combination of ingredients and, thus, produces an original and wonderful flavor. Miso is Japanese fermented soybean paste that can be found in most groceries.

Serves
4 to 6

1	tablespoon vegetable oil
1	stalk lemongrass, split lengthwise
2	cups freshly squeezed orange juice
½	bay leaf
1	teaspoon white or yellow Miso mixed with 2 cups water
1	cup apple cider
5	pounds strawberries, hulled and halved
½	cup packed mint leaves
½	cup honey
2	tablespoons sugar
1	vanilla bean, split lengthwise
2	cups Chardonnay, or other dry white wine
1	cup plain yogurt

Heat the oil in a large saucepan over medium heat. Add the lemongrass, cover and lower the heat. Cook for 5 minutes. Add the orange juice, bay leaf, miso, cider and half the strawberries. Cover and cook at a low simmer for 20 minutes. Remove from the heat and cool slightly. Purée in a blender or food processor, the 1 strain through a fine sieve; set aside.

Purée the remaining strawberries, honey and mint in the blender, then strain through a sieve. Add to the cooked strawberry mixture. Chill thoroughly.

While the soup is chilling, combine the sugar, vanilla bean and wine in a saucepan. Bring to a boil over high heat and simmer until the mixture is reduced to 1 cup. Cool and strain the sauce into a small bowl, then add the yogurt and mix well. Serve the soup chilled, garnished with swirls of the Chardonnay sauce.

Courtesy of the Fourth Story

Cucumber Vichyssoise

Cold potato-leek soup is called *vichyssoise* when it is served cold. This recipe adds another popular item from the farmers' market – the refreshing cucumber. This soup is perfect for lunch or a light supper on a hot summer day. The soup tastes the best if it is chilled overnight.

Serves
4 to 6

3   cups peeled, chopped potatoes
5   cups chicken or vegetable broth
3   cups sliced leeks (white part only)
1   small onion, chopped
2   tablespoons butter
1   large Munson cucumber, or other cucumber, peeled, seeded and chopped
1½ cups heavy cream or half & half
Salt and white pepper
Chopped fresh chives for garnish

Put the potatoes and broth in a large saucepan over medium heat. Bring to a boil, then lower the heat to a simmer. Cover and cook the potatoes for 20 minutes, or until tender. While the potatoes are cooking, melt the butter in a large skillet and add the leeks and onions. Cook over medium-low heat until the leeks are soft. When the potatoes are tender, add the cucumber, leeks and onions to the potatoes in the pot; stir to combine.

Purée the cucumber and the cooked leeks, onions and potatoes together in a blender or food processor. Return the purée to the saucepan and stir in the cream. Refrigerate the soup until cold (ideally overnight). Season with salt and white pepper once the soup is chilled. Serve cold, topped with fresh chives.

Courtesy of Munson Farms

Winter Squash

Among the anticipated flavors of autumn are the hard-shelled squash we refer to as winter squash. There are many varieties available, including butternut, delicata, acorn, red kuri and kabocha squash, as well as sugar or pie pumpkins. All of these are relatives of the zucchini-like summer squash, but most similarities end there.

Winter squash, which all have an armor-like casing, possess a dry, dense flesh ranging in color from pale yellow to intense rusty orange. Unlike their summer sisters, winter squash need to stay on the vine until fully mature. As a result, their flesh seems to be concentrated with the flavors of sugar, earth and sun.

Of all the varieties, acorn and butternut squash are probably the most familiar. Their tastes are roughly similar, but the bowling pin-shaped butternut yields far more flesh and is much easier to work with when a recipe calls for cubes, chunks or slices. Because of their pumpkin-like roundness, varieties like the acorn squash need to be hollowed out to remove the stringy membrane and seeds. Butternut squash, on the other hand, has its seeds contained in a very small area of the bottom bulb and is ready to use with little effort.

Low in calories and rich in nutrients, squash is available through the end of the market season. Size is of little importance in determining quality, as long as the squash is both heavy for its size and hard. Any softness indicates that the flesh has begun to rot, and the squash should be discarded. Market-fresh squash will last for weeks stored at room temperature.

Squash seem to have a place in nearly every cuisine. They are versatile and combine well with many other flavors. Squash can be featured in soups, stews, gratins and desserts, as well as risotto and pasta. Cut in chunks and simmered with beans, corn and a touch of chile, it has sustained generations of Native Americans.

Curried Butternut Squash Soup / Serves 8 to 10

"Ask the Chef," the Cooking School of the Rockies' booth at the Boulder County Farmers' Market, provides a unique service to visitors and farmers alike. Their chef offers cooking advice and free recipes to match the produce and ingredients of the week. Come visit them on Saturdays throughout the market season. This soup can be served hot or cold. You may substitute nearly any vegetable for the squash, including carrots or broccoli. Joan Brett, owner of Cooking School of the Rockies, says of the soup, "It's simple and delicious, but depends heavily on fresh vegetables, high-quality curry powder and good, clear chicken broth."

4   tablespoons butter
4   large shallots, minced
2   cloves garlic, minced
1   tablespoon high-quality curry powder
2½ pounds butternut squash, peeled, seeded and diced
4   cups chicken or vegetable broth, or more
Salt and white pepper
Nonfat plain yogurt to garnish
Minced fresh mint to garnish

Melt the butter in a large, heavy saucepan over medium-low heat. Add the shallots, garlic and curry powder. Cook for 3 minutes, stirring constantly. Add the squash and combine well. Cover and cook over low heat, stirring occasionally, until the onion is tender, about 15 minutes.

Add the broth to the squash mixture. Cover and simmer for 30 minutes, until the squash is tender. Cool slightly, then purée in batches in a blender or food processor. Return the soup to the saucepan and heat until the soup is very hot. Season to taste with salt and white pepper (if serving the soup cold, season with salt and pepper after it is chilled). Ladle into warm soup bowls and top with a dollop of yogurt and a sprinkling of mint.

Article courtesy of Sean Kelly, Claire de Lune; Recipe courtesy of Cooking School of the Rockies

Thai Pumpkin Soup

This unique soup is from Marcy Munson of Munson Farms. Fresh pumpkins are available in the fall and winter. In general, smaller pumpkins are more tender and have better flavor. Use pie pumpkin in the recipe – jack-o'-lantern pumpkin is too stringy. If pie pumpkin is unavailable, you can use butternut squash instead. Whole pumpkins keep at room temperature for about one month, or refrigerated for up to three months. Shrimp paste can be found in Asian markets or in the Asian section of some groceries.

Serves 4

2	tablespoons olive oil
1	large clove garlic, minced
4	shallots, minced
2	small red Thai or serrano chiles, seeded and minced (or ½ teaspoon red pepper flakes)
½	teaspoon shrimp paste
3	cups chicken or vegetable broth
1	small (2-pound) pie pumpkin, peeled, seeded and cut into ½-inch dice
1	14-ounce can coconut milk
½	pound medium shrimp, peeled and deveined
1	tablespoon minced fresh basil

In a large saucepan, heat the olive oil. Add the garlic and shallots; cook until almost soft, but not browned. Add the chiles and shrimp paste. Cook, stirring, for 1 minute.

Add the broth and pumpkin. Bring to a boil, then lower the heat so that the mixture is barely bubbling. Cover the pan and simmer for 15 minutes.

Stir in the coconut milk and simmer, covered, for another 10 minutes, or until the pumpkin is tender (up to this point, the soup may be prepared several hours before serving and refrigerated).

Heat the soup to the boiling point. Add the shrimp and cook over medium heat until the shrimp are done, about five minutes. Ladle the soup into 4 warm bowls and serve topped with a little minced basil.

Courtesy of Munson Farms

White Corn Soup with Poblano Chile Purée

You will love this combination of chiles, onions and sweet corn, accented by fresh cilantro. The chile purée can be made up to one day ahead. Keep it covered and refrigerated. Bring the purée to room temperature before serving. If white corn is unavailable, you can substitute another sweet corn variety.

Serves
4 to 6

1	large poblano chile, roasted, peeled, seeded and chopped
1	tablespoon plus 2½ cups chicken or vegetable broth, plus more if needed
3	tablespoons butter
¾	cup chopped onion
5	cups Munson white corn kernels (about 5 medium ears)

Salt and white pepper
4-6 tablespoons heavy cream
¼ cup chopped fresh cilantro

Purée the chile in a blender with 1 tablespoon of broth.

Melt the butter in a large, heavy saucepan over medium-low heat. Add the onion and cook until tender, about 10 minutes. Add the corn and cook for 2 minutes. Add the 2½ cups of broth and bring to a boil. Reduce the heat and simmer until the corn is tender, about 6 minutes. Cool slightly and then purée the soup in batches in a blender or food processor.

Return the puréed soup to the saucepan and season with salt and pepper. Reheat the soup (if it's too thick, add more broth). Ladle the soup into warm bowls. Top with a dollop of the chile purée and a dollop of cream; swirl decoratively with the tines of a fork or a knife. Sprinkle with cilantro.

Courtesy of Munson Farms

Raspberries

A recent berry-picking expedition with my son taught me an important lesson about the people who grow and sell raspberries at the farmers' market: they make their money the old-fashioned way – they earn it!

My son and I picked six pints in forty-five minutes, which I thought was pretty good, until I realized that my friend Gail, a berry grower, single-handedly picks upwards of 60 pints each market day! And though I wouldn't allow myself to complain, I definitely noticed the pain in my back as I looked over, under, around and through all those vines to find the berries. The stickers on the vines are there for a reason – to protect the berries from predators – and I was the predator ... ouch! Each berry must be handled gingerly to avoid crushing, so picking is slow going. Yes, I gained new admiration for berry pickers!

Though we did enjoy our picking expedition, I find it much easier to purchase fresh, tenderly cared for berries at the farmers' market. Buying the berries is simple, choosing what to do with them when you get them home is another matter. There are so many ways to use your raspberries, and all of them are delicious! If you want to use them fresh, simply keep them in their little pint basket in the refrigerator. Use them up quickly, since they are very delicate and won't last longer than a few days. Rinse the berries gently under cool, running water before eating. Raspberries in the refrigerator seem to call to you in the living room…the only solution is to grab a small bowlful and eat them plain, or with milk, or on top of ice cream. Once you've succumbed to that temptation, you can feel better about using your berries in recipes!

You can make a simple, versatile raspberry sauce in a jiffy by bringing 1½ cups raspberries, 1 tablespoon water and 3 teaspoons sugar to a boil. Mix 2 teaspoons cornstarch with 1 tablespoon water, add it to the berry mixture and boil for one minute longer. Strain the seeds if desired. This sauce will keep for a couple of weeks in the refrigerator and can be spooned over ice cream, used on pancakes and waffles, layered with vanilla pudding in pretty parfait glasses (my favorite). And need I say that it is a perfect partner for anything chocolate?!

To freeze berries, simply rinse briefly under cold water, drain and place on a baking sheet. Freeze until firm, then store airtight in the freezer. The berries can be used anytime for jams, pies, smoothies, muffins, cakes, and cobblers.

Article courtesy of Laura Korth, Longmont Farmers' Market

BREAKFAST & BRUNCH

Apple Coffee Cake

This is a moist, not-too-sweet cake that freezes well. It's perfect for a morning treat or a lunch-time picnic.

Serves 12

⅔   cup butter, at room temperature; plus 1 stick butter, chilled
2   cups sugar
2   eggs
2   teaspoons vanilla
3   cups plus ¼ cup flour
2   teaspoons baking soda
Pinch of salt
4   cups peeled, cored and chopped apples
1   cup chopped walnuts
½   cup packed brown sugar

Preheat the oven to 350°F. Cream together the ⅔ cup butter and sugar. Add the eggs one at a time, beating after each. Add the vanilla and blend well. In a separate bowl, mix the 3 cups of flour, baking soda and salt, then add to the butter mixture. Add the apples and nuts; mix well. Spread the batter evenly into a greased 9x13-inch baking pan.

In a small bowl, mix ¼ cup of flour and the brown sugar together. Cut the 1 stick of chilled butter into small pieces and blend in with the flour mixture. Sprinkle over the cake. Bake for 40 minutes, or until a knife inserted into the center of the cake comes out clean.

Courtesy of Ela Family Farms

Honey Granola

In addition to a complete line of honey products, J&J Apiaries offers beeswax candles and crafts. They sell their products primarily at farmers' markets and holiday shows. This granola is not too sweet and is a great source of energy while skiing, camping or hiking.

Makes
8 cups

4	cups rolled oats (not instant oats)
2	cups coarsely chopped nuts, such as cashews or pecans
1	cup golden raisins
¾	cup honey
1	stick butter
2	teaspoons cinnamon
1	teaspoon vanilla

Dash of salt

Preheat the oven to 350°F. Combine the oats, nuts and raisins in a large bowl; mix well and set aside.

Combine the honey, butter, cinnamon, vanilla and salt in a saucepan. Bring to a boil over high heat and cook for 1 minute. Pour the honey mixture over the oat mixture and toss until blended. Spread the granola evenly on a lightly greased baking sheet.

Bake for 20 minutes, stirring every 5 minutes, until lightly browned. Remove from the oven. When the mixture is completely cooled, crumble it. Store at room temperature in an airtight container for up to 1 week.

Courtesy of J&J Apiaries

Apple Breakfasts

Ahhh, autumn! The wonderful aromas that come from the autumn kitchen seem to draw us like a magnet. Is there anything quite as satisfying as turning out healthy, tasty treats for family and friends? And nothing seems to epitomize the tastes of the fall season quite like apples.

Colorado's Western Slope apples are delicious and plentiful during the months of August, September and October. If you've never had an apple "fresh off the tree," then you have a treat awaiting you!

Farmers' markets offer you the chance to sample different varieties and choose the right apple for the right recipe. Talk to the growers and tell them what you want. Are you looking for a pie apple, an eating apple with just the right blend of sweet to tart or a good "saucing" apple? The marketeers will help you find the best apple for your needs, and you'll have fun and get an education in the process.

As mornings become chilly, I conjure up visions of hot, hearty breakfasts enjoyed with the whole family seated around the table. However, like many families, reality is somewhat different than my vision. The troops start heading out the door at 6 a.m., with no time to eat because they preferred to catch a few more minutes of precious sleep.

As a result, we eat a goodly number of on-the-run breakfasts, which is fine, as long as they are made with wholesome ingredients. In addition, they must be quick and easy enough for a fuzzy brain (mine) to fix.

When you include apples in your breakfasts, you are not only giving your family something that tastes good and is good for them, but the wonderful aroma coming from the kitchen will get them rolling out of bed. Here are some quick, delicious breakfast ideas that make great use of our Colorado apples:

• Lightly toast thick slices of whole wheat bread. Spread with cream cheese. Lay thinly sliced sweet apples (such as Golden Delicious or Gala) on top. Sprinkle with sugar and cinnamon. Broil until the sugar is brown and bubbly.

• Place sautéed apple slices (see recipe below) on a lightly toasted English muffin or bagel and top with a slice of cheese (and a slice of ham, if desired). Broil until the cheese is bubbly.

• Fill a warm tortilla with sautéed apple slices. Fold up like a burrito. You can wrap these in foil and keep them warm in the oven so everyone can grab one or two as they head out the door.

• Spread whole wheat toast with peanut or almond butter. Top with applesauce.

Sautéed Apple Slices / Serves 2 to 4

These can be made the night before and refrigerated, then reheated in the morning. These apples are good used in the ideas noted above, or as a tasty accompaniment for a weekend breakfast of waffles and sausage.

2   tart apples, washed, peeled, quartered and cored
2   tablespoons sugar
¼   teaspoon cinnamon
⅛   teaspoon nutmeg
2   tablespoons butter

Cut the apples into ¼-inch slices. Combine the sugar, cinnamon and nutmeg.

Melt the butter in a skillet over medium heat. Add the apples and stir to coat. Sauté the apples for 4 minutes, stirring occasionally so they don't burn. Pour the sugar mixture into the pan and stir the apples to coat. Cook for 1 minute more. Serve warm.

Courtesy of Laura Korth, Longmont Farmers' Market

Garden-Tot Scramble

Denver Urban Gardens (DUG) was established in 1985 to develop and support community gardens. DUG quickly diversified its projects to include small parks and habitat education gardens. DUG has since expanded across the city. In 1998, a training program was started, focusing on environmental and horticulture education for underserved and disadvantaged youth and adults. By 2000, DUG was serving nearly 70 active gardens and nine park and outdoor "habitat classrooms" across metro Denver. This recipe was the hit of a recent spring brunch. "Morning Star Crumblers" used in the recipe are a vegetarian bulk sausage. The recipe was tested with turkey sausage with delicious results.

Serves 6

1	32-ounce bag Tater Tots
1	bag Morning Star Crumblers (or 1 pound turkey or pork breakfast sausage)
2	tablespoons olive oil
2	cloves garlic, crushed
⅛	teaspoon cayenne
1	cup chopped red onion
1	small zucchini, chopped
2	avocados, chopped
2	tomatoes, peeled and chopped
1	cup grated Pepper Jack or sharp cheddar cheese

Bake Tater Tots as directed. Heat 1 tablespoon of oil in a large skillet. Add the garlic, Crumblers or sausage and cayenne. Cook until browned, then remove from the pan and set aside.

Heat 1 tablespoon of oil in the pan used to cook the Crumblers. Add the onion and cook until soft. Add the zucchini and cook until crisp-tender. Add the tater tots and Crumblers; heat through, breaking up the tater tots, if desired. Add the cheese and stir to melt. Serve with avocado, tomato and salsa.

Courtesy of Denver Urban Gardens

Pear Walnut Coffee Cake

This is a delicious, simple coffee cake that is not too sweet. It would also be good with peaches, raspberries or apples in place of the pears.

Serves
8 to 10

1	stick margarine
¾	cup sugar
1	teaspoon vanilla
1	egg
2	cups flour
1	teaspoon baking soda
1	teaspoon baking powder
½	teaspoon salt
1	cup plain yogurt
3	cups peeled, chopped pears (about 4 pears)
1	cup packed brown sugar
1½	teaspoons cinnamon
½	stick butter, at room temperature
1	cup chopped walnuts

Preheat the oven to 350°F. Cream the margarine and sugar together. Stir in the vanilla and egg. Add the flour, baking soda, baking powder and salt alternately with the yogurt. Fold in the pears. Pour into an 8x8-inch or 9x9-inch baking pan.

Combine the brown sugar, cinnamon, butter and walnuts in a small bowl; sprinkle over the batter. Bake for 40 to 50 minutes, or until a knife inserted in the center comes out clean.

Courtesy of First Fruits Organic Farms

Zucchini Frittata

A frittata is an Italian omelet. The main difference between a frittata and an omelet is that the frittata has the ingredients mixed with the eggs instead of being placed inside the fold of the omelet. Also, a frittata is not cooked as fast as an omelet. This recipe calls for the frittata to be baked, but you can also cook it in a cast iron skillet on the stove. The following recipe makes a savory brunch dish, and is also ideal for a light, late summer supper.

Serves
4 to 6

2	tablespoons olive oil
1	onion, chopped
1	clove garlic, minced
1½	cups coarsely grated zucchini (or yellow squash or a combination)
1	tomato, peeled and chopped
½	cup bread crumbs
½	teaspoon chopped fresh thyme
1	tablespoon chopped fresh parsley
½	cup grated Parmesan cheese
6-8	eggs, beaten

Preheat the oven to 350°F. Grease a 9x9-inch baking pan. Heat the oil in a large skillet, add the onions and cook until soft. Add the garlic and stir briefly. Put the onion and garlic in a medium mixing bowl. Add the zucchini, tomato, bread crumbs, thyme, parsley and cheese; mix well. Stir in the eggs.

Pour the egg mixture into the prepared baking dish or an oven-proof skillet and bake for 25 to 30 minutes, until the top is light golden brown. Serve the frittata in squares (or wedges if using round skillet) with a salad and corn bread, or cut into smaller squares for appetizers.

Courtesy of Laura Korth, Longmont Farmers' Market

Raspberry French Toast

Straw Hat Farm is a 15-acre farm that has been certified organic since 1997. In addition to growing vegetables and raspberries, the farm also raises Boer goats. This French toast will bring rave reviews at your next breakfast or brunch. Note: the dish needs to be refrigerated overnight.

Serves 4

6	slices bread (use your favorite), cut into 1-inch cubes
1	8-ounce package cream cheese, cut into 1-inch cubes
1	cup fresh or frozen raspberries
6	eggs
1	cup milk
⅓	cup maple syrup

Raspberry sauce, warmed (recipe follows)

Put half the bread cubes into a greased 8x8-inch baking pan. Top the bread with the cream cheese cubes, then top with the raspberries and remaining bread cubes.

In a mixing bowl, beat the eggs, milk and syrup. Pour the egg mixture over the bread mixture. Cover with foil and chill for 8 hours, or overnight. Remove from the refrigerator 30 minutes before baking.

Preheat the oven to 350°F. Put the French toast into the oven and bake, covered with foil, for 30 minutes. Uncover and bake for 20 to 30 minutes more, until the mixture is golden brown and the center is set. Divide among 4 warm plates and drizzle with the warm raspberry sauce. Serve with extra warm raspberry sauce.

For the raspberry sauce:

1	cup sugar
2	tablespoons cornstarch
1	cup water
1	cup fresh raspberries (or use frozen raspberries, thawed)
1	tablespoon butter

In a saucepan, combine the sugar and cornstarch. Add the water and stir until the cornstarch has dissolved. Bring to the mixture to a boil. Boil for 3 minutes, stirring constantly. Stir in the raspberries and boil for 1 minute more. Remove from the heat. Add the butter and stir until it is melted and combined. Serve warm.

Courtesy of Straw Hat Farm

Hearty Breakfast Casserole

The two major types of potatoes grown in Colorado's San Luis Valley are russets and reds. The familiar russet is an oval shaped, brown skinned, smooth textured potato. The Red Sangre is a red potato developed in the San Luis Valley. A third potato with a smaller crop but a growing reputation is the Yukon Gold. It has a yellow skin and flesh with sweet flavor. This casserole is a simple egg and potato dish, with the addition of your choice of ham, sausage or bacon, and red bell pepper for flavor and color. For a Southwestern touch, serve it with sour cream and salsa, and garnish with sprigs of cilantro.

Serves
4 to 6

2-3 large Colorado russet potatoes, peeled and thinly sliced
Salt and black pepper
8 ounces bulk low-fat sausage, 6 ounces finely chopped lean ham
or 6 ounces turkey bacon, cooked and crumbled
⅓ cup chopped roasted red bell pepper or 2-ounce jar pimentos, chopped
3 eggs
1 cup low-fat milk
3 tablespoons minced chives or green onion tops

Preheat the oven to 375°F. Butter an 8x8-inch or 9x9-inch baking pan, or other small, oven-proof casserole dish. Arrange half the potatoes in the baking pan. Sprinkle with salt and pepper. Cover with half the meat. Arrange the remaining potatoes on top and sprinkle with salt and pepper. Top with the other half of the meat and the red peppers.

Whisk the eggs, milk and chives until well-blended. Pour the egg mixture over the potatoes. Cover the baking dish with foil and bake for 45 to 50 minutes, until the potatoes are tender. Uncover and bake for 10 minutes more. Divide among 4 to 6 warm plates and serve immediately.

Courtesy of Colorado Potato Administrative Committee

SIDE DISHES

Beets

One sign that American cuisine has evolved over the last decade or so is the increased consumption of beets. It once seemed that beets only came from a can and were used solely for filling space on a steak-house salad bar. Sometime during the food revolution of the '80s, chefs began experimenting with fresh ingredients that had formerly been overlooked, such as the lowly beet. One creative chef took small beets – about the size of radishes – roasted them and sliced them into a field green salad. The beet's image has never been quite the same.

Unlike some other baby vegetables, small beets are especially luscious and packed with sweetness. Although most folks think of beets only in their crimson shade, they can also be found in gold and candy-stripe (also known as Chioggia) varieties. Both of these alternatives are slightly sweeter and therefore more prized. Any color will taste great though, as long as one always tries to buy beets that are not too much larger in size than an egg or a lemon. Whenever possible, buy beets with their greens still attached. Beet greens, like the roots, are a great source of nutrients. They're similar in taste to Swiss chard and can be cooked in the same manner, perhaps braised with a little olive oil and some lemon for an easy side dish.

Beets can be stored for several weeks. To store, separate the beets from their greens and place the beets in a plastic bag in the refrigerator. Roasted beets should last for a week if stored airtight in the refrigerator. Beet greens should be handled and stored like other greens. Locally grown beets are great tasting, nutritious and easy to prepare – all that we look for in today's food choices.

Roasted Beets / Serves 4 to 6

Roasting gives beets an entirely different flavor than when you boil or steam them. Serve these delicious beets sliced into your favorite salad or serve as a component of an antipasto plate. For an excellent summer salad, try pairing roasted beets with local greens, onions, fresh herb vinaigrette and either Haystack Mountain ricotta salata or Bingham Hill blue cheese.

1½ tablespoons olive oil
1   teaspoon salt
3   bunches (12 to 15) small beets, trimmed and scrubbed
2   tablespoons balsamic vinegar (optional)

Preheat the oven to 400°F. Put the oil, salt and beets in a stainless steel bowl and toss to coat. Put the beets in an oven-proof skillet or baking pan. Add about ¼-inch of water, then pour the vinegar over the top. Cover tightly with foil and bake for approximately 1 hour, or until the beets are fairly soft when stuck with a toothpick. Allow the beets to cool, then peel them and they are ready to serve.

Article and recipe courtesy of Sean Kelly, Claire de Lune

Sugar Snap Peas with Mint

The beautiful thing about using fresh farmers' market peas is that they don't have to be cooked. They come sweet and perfect! Prepare these peas just before you are ready to sit down and enjoy your meal.

Serves 2

2 tablespoons butter
1-2 cups fresh sugar snap peas
1 tablespoon finely chopped mint
Salt and black pepper

Melt the butter in a skillet over medium-high heat. Add the peas and cook until the peas just turn bright green – they shouldn't be raw, but should be crisp. Toss in the chopped mint and season with salt and pepper. Serve immediately.

Courtesy of Potager

Roasted Bell Peppers

The basic procedure for roasting peppers is described here. The roasted peppers can be served as a side dish or as an ingredient in many recipes. Or use them as a topping for burgers or pizza. This dish is a simple, but delicious way to enjoy bell peppers. The longer the peppers sit, the better the flavor. For a little more pizzazz, try a splash of balsamic or flavored vinegar.

Serves 2

4-5 organic red, green and/or yellow bell peppers
3 tablespoons olive oil
1 clove garlic, minced
Freshly ground black pepper

Preheat the oven to 350°F. Place the peppers on a greased baking sheet and roast for 20 to 30 minutes, turning every 5 minutes until the skin of the entire pepper is evenly blistered.

Immediately place the roasted peppers in a brown paper bag. Fold down the top to seal the bag and let the peppers steam for 5 minutes. Remove the peppers and peel off the skin. Cut out the stems and seeds and slice the peppers into strips.

Combine the oil, garlic and black pepper; mix with the roasted peppers. Let sit for at least 1 hour before serving or using.

Courtesy of Front Range Organic Gardeners

Sweet Potato Pie

Sunshine Farms is a registered Community Supported Agricultural (CSA) farm. You can find their produce and herbs at Colorado farmers' markets and a select few Durango restaurants (in season, of course). "Here on Sunshine Farms, we produce locally, to provide locally," says Rachel Bowers of Sunshine Farms. "This is my favorite family holiday recipe. Typically, I double the recipe as leftovers prove to be just as delicious."

Serves
4 to 6

3	tablespoons butter, at room temperature
2	tablespoons sugar
2	eggs, beaten
3	cups peeled, cooked and mashed sweet potatoes
⅓	cup milk
1	teaspoon vanilla
½	cup packed brown sugar
¼	cup flour
½	cup chopped pecans (or other favorite nuts)

Preheat the oven to 350°F. Melt 1 tablespoon of butter. Combine the sugar, eggs, sweet potatoes, milk, melted butter and vanilla in a large bowl; mix well, then transfer to a glass or ceramic baking dish.

In another bowl, mix the brown sugar, 2 tablespoons of butter, flour and nuts. Sprinkle on top of the sweet potato mixture. Bake, uncovered, for 25 to 30 minutes, or until the topping is browned.

Courtesy of Sunshine Farms

New Potatoes

New potatoes are freshly dug, young potatoes of any variety or, technically speaking, potatoes harvested while the leaves are still green and full. The fresh, delicately sweet flavor of new potatoes is never forgotten. A simple preparation is all they need to be thoroughly enjoyed. Their skin is so thin and tender, they need not even be peeled. After boiling or steaming new potatoes until tender, toss them with a little butter, some minced chive and a few sprinklings of sea salt.

Over the last decade, Americans' appreciation for potato varieties – other than the traditional russets – has blossomed. The farmers of the San Luis Valley (where most of Colorado's potatoes are grown) seem to be giving all of them a try. At any given market, you will find different sizes of such varieties as creamers, Peruvian Purples, fingerlings, Yellow Finns and the ever-popular red skinned new potato.

Potatoes, in general, are versatile, with their size and starch content being the most important factors in determining their best use. Creamers and purple potatoes are best suited for boiling, while fingerlings are better roasted whole, in their skins. Red skins and Yellow Finns are perfect for either preparation.

Look for potatoes that are rock hard with no sprouts or large eyes, and absolutely no green tinting to the skin. Freshly harvested new potatoes will last for four to seven days if stored loosely in a brown paper bag in the cupboard. However, their qualities will begin to dissipate after a couple of days. Refrigeration is not recommended for potatoes as it accelerates the aging process. Potatoes should be washed thoroughly just before using them.

Killer BBQ Potatoes / Serves 4

The best way to cook these potatoes is to grill them, but they may also be roasted in a very hot oven. If you roast them, they do not have to be parboiled first. Use the smallest new potatoes you can find at the market for the best result.

2	pounds new potatoes
1	medium onion, chopped
2	tablespoons olive oil
1½	cups ketchup
½	cup packed dark brown sugar
1	teaspoon salt
½	teaspoon dry mustard
3	large cloves garlic, minced
1½	cups water
1	tablespoon Worcestershire sauce
¼	teaspoon Tabasco
¼	teaspoon cayenne pepper
2	teaspoons Liquid Smoke
1	teaspoon cider vinegar
½	teaspoon black pepper

Butter
Salt and black pepper

Put the onions and oil in a large saucepan over medium heat. Cook the onions until they are not quite tender. Add the ketchup, brown sugar, salt, dry mustard, garlic, water, Worcestershire, Tabasco, cayenne, Liquid Smoke, vinegar and pepper and mix. Lower the heat slightly and simmer the sauce for 20 minutes or more.

Fill a large saucepan with lightly salted water and bring to a boil. Add the potatoes and boil for about 10 minutes. The first quarter of the potatoes should look cooked when halved. Drain.

Grill the potatoes over very hot coals (or roast them in a very hot oven), turning often, until a crust has formed on the outside and they are tender inside. While the potatoes are cooking, generously baste them with more sauce. When the potatoes are done, quickly halve or quarter them and place them in a large bowl. Toss with butter, salt and pepper. Serve with extra barbecue sauce, if desired.

Article courtesy of Sean Kelly, Claire de Lune; Recipe courtesy of Janis Judd, Editor

Finocchio al Pesto (Baked Fennel with Pesto)

Fennel, which is believed to aid in digestion, is very popular in Italy. It's slightly anise taste adds a unique flavor to savory dishes. Baked fennel with Pesto is very simple to prepare but looks and tastes like something you slaved for hours to make. Loredana's Casalinga Pesto is a classic pesto. Durango Pesto is a spicy pesto with cilantro and jalapeño. Citrus Pesto has orange and lime juice instead of oil.

Serves 4 to 6

2	pounds fennel bulbs, halved and rinsed
½	stick butter, cut into small pieces
1	6.5-ounce container Loredana's Casalinga, Durango or Citrus Pesto, or other favorite pesto
⅓	cup grated Parmesan cheese

In a large saucepan of boiling water, cook the fennel until it is just tender. Drain and cool.

Preheat the oven to 400°F. Cut the fennel bulbs lengthwise into 4 or 6 wedges. Arrange them in a buttered baking dish. Dot the fennel with butter and pesto. Sprinkle with Parmesan cheese and bake until the cheese is golden brown, about 20 minutes.

Courtesy of Loredana's Pesto

Asian Spinach with Oranges and Sesame Seeds

Established in the mid-1970s, Grant Family Farms is the largest organic farm in Colorado. The farm produces a multitude of vegetables and grains, but they are known for their spinach and squashes. Use Grant Farms organic Savoy spinach for this dish when it is in season in late April or early May.

Serves 4 to 6

1	tablespoon olive oil
2	large bunches fresh spinach (about 1¼ pounds), trimmed and thoroughly washed, but not dried
⅓	cup chicken or vegetable broth
1	tablespoon low-sodium soy sauce
½	teaspoon sugar
2	oranges, peeled and cut into bite-size pieces
1	tablespoon toasted sesame seeds

Heat the oil in a large saucepan over medium heat. Add the damp spinach and cook, covered, for 4 to 5 minutes, stirring occasionally, until the leaves are just wilted. Drain well and set aside.

In the same pot, combine the broth, soy sauce and sugar. Bring to boil. Reduce the heat to low, stir in the spinach and orange pieces and heat through. Sprinkle sesame seeds over the top and serve immediately with additional soy sauce.

Courtesy of Grant Family Farms

Pesto Corn on the Cob

It is difficult to imagine getting tired of just plain buttered corn on the cob, but this variation is a good change of pace. It is an updated take on an old-fashioned, family picnic favorite.

Serves 6

6 ears corn, husks and silk removed
¼ cup Loredana's Casalinga or Durango Pesto, or other favorite pesto
½ stick butter
1 cup grated Parmesan cheese
Black pepper

Preheat the oven to 400°F. Bring a large stockpot full of water to boil over high heat. Cook the corn in boiling water for 4 minutes. While the corn is cooking, melt the butter and combine it with the pesto (more or less to your taste).

Spread the butter-pesto mixture on the corn. Roll the ears in Parmesan cheese and sprinkle with freshly ground black pepper. Wrap the corn in foil and bake in the oven for 10 minutes. Serve immediately.

Courtesy of Loredana's Pesto

Green Beans

Our high altitude growing season does not reach its peak until the end of July but when it finally in full swing, the market choices are nearly overwhelming. Green or yellow (even purple) beans are in abundance. Like all other vegetables, green beans are at their best when purchased from the farmers' market, having been picked just 24 to 48 hours before. Green bean quality diminishes rapidly soon after they have been harvested, with a loss of flavor and crispness occurring within days.

Aside from freshness, the other key factor in determining quality is size. As beans get longer and fatter, their flavor suffers and their texture gets tougher. This is why most chefs favor haricots verts, the petite, thin French bean. However, most haricot vert are grown so far from here that their fine qualities may be lost with time and travel. Therefore, locally grown, crisp, blemish-free and not-too-large green beans rule, and should be used both for immediate consumption and for canning.

Although these beans go by such names as snap beans, wax beans and string beans, they are all relatively similar in taste (with yellow wax beans being slightly larger and starchier than the green varieties). Their strings have been bred out, so the only trimming required is to snap off the stem end. Removing the point end is a matter of choice. The trimming allows water to enter the bean for a faster, more thorough cooking process. Beans should not be trimmed until the time of use. Most recipes call for beans to be blanched in salted boiling water, then shocked in ice water to cool, as a preliminary step. Doing this ahead is fine, although flavor is maximized if the blanching is done right before the beans go into the dish, as in the recipe below.

Green beans, rich in potassium and high in fiber, are in season from July until frost, but are at their best early in their season. Many farmers grow beans in bi-weekly succession so that high-quality, young beans are always coming to market. Look for crisp, clean, small beans. Store them in a plastic bag for up to one week. Like most vegetables in summer's bounty, green beans go well with other vegetables, herbs and cheeses. They might be at their best, though, when served warm, paired with a hearty dollop of aïoli (a garlic-flavored mayonnaise sauce from Provence).

Green Beans Braised with Tomato and Rosemary / Serves 4

This dish is excellent with grilled tuna or chicken. Many vendors at the farmers' markets, such as The Fresh Herb Company, sell potted rosemary plants, which provide a convenient, year-round herb source. You can boil the green beans ahead of time. Just have them at room temperature when you are ready to continue.

1   pound green beans, trimmed
½   cup olive oil
½   cup sliced onion
2-3 cloves garlic, minced
1   medium tomato, peeled and chopped
1½   tablespoons chopped fresh rosemary
Salt and black pepper

Bring 6 quarts of salted water to a boil. Add the beans and simmer, uncovered, until just tender, about 4 minutes. If you want the beans to keep their bright green color, drain them and plunge them into ice water, then drain again as soon as the beans have cooled.

While the beans are simmering, heat the oil in a skillet. Add the onion and cook over medium-high heat until translucent. Add the garlic, and cook for 1 minute, stirring to avoid burning. Reduce the heat to medium-low. Drain the beans and add directly to the onion and garlic. Add the tomatoes and rosemary. Cover and simmer for 5 minutes. Add salt and pepper to taste. Serve hot or at room temperature.

Recipe and article courtesy of Sean Kelly, Claire de Lune

Grilled New Potatoes and Greens

Gorgonzola Dolce is a slightly sweet, softer Gorgonzola. It is available at specialty markets. Use the smallest red-skinned potatoes available for this recipe. If only larger potatoes are available, halve them before tossing them with the cheese. The best way to cook these potatoes is to grill them over very high heat. They can also be roasted in a very hot oven, in which case they don't have to be parboiled first.

Serves 6

2   pounds new potatoes
½   pound Gorgonzola Dolce cheese, plus more to taste
4   cups arugula, washed and dried
Salt and black pepper

Fill a large saucepan with lightly salted water and bring to a boil. Add the potatoes and boil for about 10 minutes (the first ¼-inch of the potatoes should look cooked when halved). Drain the potatoes.

Grill (or roast) the potatoes over very hot coals, turning often, until a crust has formed on the outside and they are tender inside.

While the potatoes are grilling, place the Gorgonzola in a large bowl. Divide the arugula among 6 salad plates. When the potatoes are done, toss them with the cheese. Add salt and pepper to taste and serve immediately over the salad greens.

Courtesy of The Fresh Herb Company

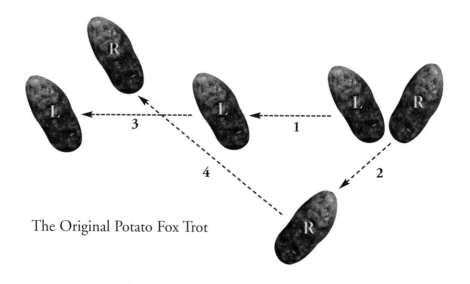

The Original Potato Fox Trot

Potato Gorgonzola Gratin

Most people do not know that Colorado is the second largest potato producing state. Most Colorado potatoes are grown high in the San Luis Valley, where one of the world's largest aquifer lies beneath the valley floor. Fed by run-off from heavy winter snowfall, the aquifer provides plentiful irrigation and pure mountain water, creating one of the best tasting potatoes grown anywhere. Apples, onions, potatoes and gorgonzola are in perfect harmony in this warming fall or winter dish.

Serves
4 to 6

1	pound unpeeled Colorado russet potatoes, thinly sliced

Salt and black pepper
Ground nutmeg

½	medium onion, thinly sliced
1	medium tart green apple or 1 pear, unpeeled, cored and thinly sliced
1	cup half & half or milk
3	ounces Gorgonzola or blue cheese, crumbled
2	tablespoons grated Parmesan cheese

Preheat the oven to 400°F. Grease an 8x8-inch or 9x9-inch baking dish, or other small casserole dish. Arrange half of the potatoes in the baking dish. Season generously with salt and pepper, then sprinkle lightly with nutmeg. Top with the onion and apple. Arrange the remaining potatoes on top. Season again with salt and pepper. Pour the half & half over the potatoes and cover the dish with foil. Bake for 35 to 40 minutes, until the potatoes are tender. Remove the foil and top with the cheeses. Bake uncovered for 10 to 15 minutes, until the top is lightly browned.

Courtesy of Colorado Potato Administrative Committee

Curried Quinoa

2	tablespoons sesame oil
1	clove garlic, minced
1	small onion, finely chopped
½	cup chopped red bell pepper
½	cup peas
1	teaspoon curry powder
3	cups water
2	cups quinoa

Yogurt to garnish
Chutney to garnish

Heat the oil in a stock pot over medium heat. Cook the garlic, onion and bell pepper until soft. Lower the heat and add the peas and curry powder; cover and cook for 5 minutes. Add the water, cover and bring to a boil.

Meanwhile, toast the quinoa in a skillet for 5 minutes, stirring constantly. When the water comes to a boil, add the quinoa, turn the heat to low, cover and cook for 15 to 20 minutes, until the quinoa is done. Serve with yogurt and/or chutney.

Courtesy of Green Earth Farms

Carrot Pilaf

This is a colorful side dish with lots of flavor. For added fiber, try long grain brown rice and cook for 45 to 50 minutes.

Serves 6

1	tablespoon butter
1	cup shredded carrot
¼	cup chopped white onion
¼	cup chopped green onion
1	cup long grain rice
2	cups chicken broth
1	teaspoon lemon pepper

In a medium saucepan, melt the butter over medium heat. Add the carrots and onions; cook until crisp-tender. Add the rice and stir to mix. Add the broth and lemon pepper. Bring to a boil. Reduce heat, cover and simmer for 20 minutes, or until the rice is tender. Let sit covered for 5 minutes before serving.

Courtesy of Pueblo Farmers Marketeers

LOCAL FLAVOR

ORGANIC

Rich Abrahamson (top left); Colorado Fresh Markets/Cherry Creek Fresh Market (top right); USDA (bottom)

SUNRISE

MARKET FRESH

Bob Castellino (top left); Paul Bousquet (middle left & middle right); Colorado Fresh Markets/City Park Esplanade Fresh Market

Paul Bousquet

MOUTH
WATERING

ORCHARD

Paul Bousquet (top and bottom); USDA (middle left and middle right)

Vegetarian Mixed Grill

The Pueblo Farmers' Market is a non-profit venture operated by the Pueblo County Master Gardeners, under the name Farmers Marketeers, Inc. Profits are given to 4-H young people in the form of scholarships. The following recipe is full of market-fresh vegetables. Note: calavacitas are small, round summer squash.

Serves
4 to 6

3	small onions, halved
2	carrots, peeled
3	small pattypan or sunburst squash
1	medium green bell pepper
1	medium red bell pepper
2	small calavacitas or zucchini
¼	cup olive oil

Dash of black pepper

¾	teaspoon minced fresh marjoram, or ¼ teaspoon dried
1	teaspoon minced fresh rosemary, or ⅓ teaspoon dried

Cut all of the vegetables into 1-inch chunks. Cook the onions and carrots in a saucepan of simmering water for 10 minutes, or until crisp-tender. Drain.

In a large bowl, combine the olive oil, pepper, marjoram and rosemary. Add the vegetables and toss to coat well. Cover and refrigerate for 1 hour. Drain, reserving the marinade.

Thread the vegetables alternately onto skewers and grill over medium heat for 15 to 20 minutes, turning and basting with the reserved marinade every 4 to 5 minutes, until tender.

Courtesy of Pueblo Farmers Marketeers

Swiss Chard

Chard, commonly referred to as Swiss chard, has never enjoyed the same following in the United Stated that it has in Europe, where it has been a garden staple for centuries. In fact, it is so popular in some areas – particularly along the Mediterranean – that it can even be found in desserts. While it is difficult to envision Americans embracing chard in our dessert repertoire, it has many other uses. Chard is a healthy green with a slight, beet-like sweetness. However, it is most similar to spinach, and can be used in almost any dish in which cooked spinach would be employed.

Chard has a lengthy growing season and is available throughout the summer. The leaves are always green and should have a natural waxy shine with no blemishes or spots. The stems and veins are typically white or red (red stemmed chard is often called beet chard or rhubarb chard). There is also a variety called Bright Lights chard that has vivid red, yellow and orange coloring and streaking in the stems. Regardless the stem color, all chard varieties are roughly interchangeable in taste.

The stems of the chard should usually be removed, although there are some French preparations where you would keep the stems intact – for example, stuffed chard or gratinéed stems. Wash chard when you are ready to use it. It will keep up to one week in an air-tight plastic bag or other sealed container in the refrigerator.

Wilted Chard with Pine Nuts and Blond Raisins / Serves 4

This Sicilian-inspired side dish is excellent with full-flavored fish or grilled chicken. Plump the raisins by putting them in a small bowl and covering them with warm water for about 30 minutes to rehydrate.

1	pound chard
2	tablespoons olive oil
1	cup chopped onion
1	tablespoon minced garlic
¼	cup blond raisins, plumped
2	tablespoons red wine vinegar
2	tablespoons pine nuts, toasted

Salt and black pepper

Wash the chard and then drain it in a large colander (do not spin dry). In a large skillet, warm the oil over medium heat until just smoking. Add the onion and cook until translucent, but not browned. Add the garlic and cook, stirring, for 1 minute. Add the chard and cover the pan. Remove the cover every 30 seconds and stir the chard to facilitate wilting. When wilted, but not darkened (about 2 minutes), add the raisins and vinegar. Season with salt and pepper. Toss the mixture and taste for seasoning. Serve garnished with toasted pine nuts.

Article and recipe courtesy of Sean Kelly, Claire de Lune

Steamed Green Beans With Shiitake Mushrooms and Cheese

Serves
4 to 6

"The best vegetable recipes are the simplest," says Chet Anderson, of The Fresh Herb Company. "Choose bright green beans of uniform size. The smaller the beans are, the more tender they will be. They should 'snap' when bent." Oka is a Canadian cheese with a medium-strong taste and the consistency of a semi-hard cheese, such as fontina. It can be found at specialty markets and some groceries.

1	pound fresh green beans, or more as needed, ends snapped off
2	tablespoons butter
¼	pound shiitake mushrooms, cleaned, stemmed and sliced
¾	cup grated Oka cheese

Salt and black pepper

Put the beans in a steamer over lightly salted, boiling water. Cover the pot and steam the beans until done to your taste, about 10 minutes for crisp-tender beans.

Meanwhile, heat the butter in a small skillet. When the butter is melted and bubbling, add the mushrooms and cook until tender, about 10 minutes.

Drain the beans and place them in a warm bowl. Add the mushrooms and cheese, and toss. Add salt and pepper to taste. Serve immediately.

Courtesy of The Fresh Herb Company

Green Beans with Tarragon-Chive Butter

These green beans are delicious served with brine-cured pork chops (see page 146). The herb butter can be prepared ahead of time. All you have to do is cook the green beans and toss them with the herb butter just before serving.

Serves 4

½	stick butter, at room temperature
½	cup finely chopped mixed herbs, such as parsley, tarragon and chives

Salt and black pepper
1½ pounds young green beans

Blend or mash the butter and herbs together. Season with salt and pepper. Melt the butter in a saucepan and add the green beans. Stir to coat the beans. Cook over low heat until the beans are crisp-tender.

Courtesy of Potager

Grilled Eggplant with Shallots and Tomatoes

Lyle Davis, owner of Boulder County's Pastures of Plenty says, "My love of food and gardening came from my family and our place in the Hudson River Valley of New York. We had a beautiful 150-year-old farmhouse with four acres of gardens." Both of his parents loved to garden. "My mother was a remarkable cook," adds Davis. "I really learned to appreciate food and to love gardening from her. She loved gathering friends and family around a table. In late August, when eggplants are overtaking our fields at Pastures of Plenty, we make this dish for our harvest crew suppers."

Serves
6 to 8

2	medium eggplants, sliced into ½-inch thick rounds (you can leave the skin on if the eggplant is fresh)
1	cup olive oil
4	shallots, minced
2	lemons, juiced
1	bunch Italian parsley, finely chopped
2-3	tomatoes, peeled and chopped into ¼-inch dice

Salt and black pepper

Generously brush the eggplant with olive oil and grill on both sides, or roast in the oven (do not allow the eggplant to char). Remove the eggplant from the heat when it is soft and pliable.

In a medium skillet, heat 2 tablespoons of olive oil. Cook the shallots in the oil over medium heat until soft. Add the lemon juice, parsley (reserving a little for garnish) and tomatoes. Add salt and pepper to taste. Cook for 4 minutes, stirring occasionally. Remove from the heat.

Arrange the eggplant slices on a platter in a circle. Parallel the eggplant circle with a 2-inch band of the shallot mixture. Sprinkle with the reserved parsley. Serve warm or cold.

Courtesy of Pastures of Plenty

Calavacitas

Denver's Seasoned Chef Cooking School offers tours of the farmers' markets, followed by a class using the bounty the students gathered. This easy recipe sings with Colorado summer flavors, melding the crunch of fresh corn with buttery soft squash. Calavacitas are a small, round summer squash.

Serves
4 to 6

1	tablespoon butter
1	tablespoon olive oil
1	onion, chopped
2	cloves garlic, minced
4	ears fresh corn, kernels removed
2	medium calavacitas or zucchini, sliced
½	cup chopped roasted green chiles (fresh or canned), hot or mild
½	cup shredded fontina or Monterey Jack cheese
⅓	cup heavy cream or half & half

Salt and white pepper

Heat the butter and olive oil in a large skillet. Add the onion and cook, stirring occasionally, until tender and translucent. Stir in the garlic, corn, zucchini and green chiles. Cover and cook over low heat until the zucchini is crisp-tender, about 5 minutes. Add the cheese and cream; cover and cook for 1 to 2 minutes more, or until the cheese has melted. Season to taste with salt and white pepper and serve.

Courtesy of the Seasoned Chef Cooking School

Zucchini Fritters

These fritters make a very nice summer side dish. Try adding a couple tablespoons of seasoned bread crumbs for additional flavor and texture.

Serves 4

2	tablespoons peanut or canola oil, plus more for frying
1	large yellow onion, chopped
4-5	small to medium zucchini, coarsely grated
2	tablespoons chopped fresh basil
2	tablespoons grated Parmesan cheese
2	eggs, lightly beaten
3	tablespoons flour
½	teaspoon baking powder
1	teaspoon salt
½	teaspoon black pepper

Pinch of cayenne
Crème fraîche or sour cream to garnish

Heat the oil in a large skillet over medium heat. Add the onions and cook until translucent. Place the onions in a large mixing bowl. Cool to room temperature, then add the zucchini, basil and Parmesan; mix well. Sift the flour and baking powder together and add to the onion mixture along with the eggs, salt, pepper and cayenne. Mix well and let sit for 10 minutes.

Preheat the oven to 200°F. Heat ¼ inch of oil in a large cast iron or non-stick skillet until hot enough that a drop of water pops and sizzles. Spoon enough of the fritter batter into the oil to make 2- to 3-inch circles. With a metal spatula, flatten the fritters into disks. Fry until golden brown on both sides, about 3 minutes per side. Remove the fritters to a paper towel-lined plate and keep warm in the oven. Continue with the remaining batter. Serve the fritters warm with a dollop of crème fraîche or sour cream.

Courtesy of Sean Kelly, Claire de Lune

Spectacular Frozen Corn

Bill and Phyllis Roth have been farming east of Greeley since 1974, growing hay, sweet corn and a variety of produce. They also make pickles and have a herd of Black Angus cattle. This corn can be used immediately or frozen for later use (and will still be better than store-bought corn after corn season ends).

Makes
4 to 5 cups

10	ears fresh sweet corn, husked, silk removed and washed
1	stick butter
½	cup half & half

Salt and sugar to taste (optional)

Preheat the oven to 325°F. Cut the kernels from the corn cobs and put into a large roasting pan. Add the butter and half & half. Bake for 1 hour, stirring occasionally. Remove from the oven and mix in the optional salt and sugar.

If freezing, cool the corn, then seal it in freezer bags and freeze. To serve the frozen corn, heat it thoroughly in a saucepan.

Courtesy of Bill and Phillis Roth Farms

Roasted Asparagus with Garlic

Front Range Organic Gardeners is an organic gardening club established in 1987. The club meets monthly for educational lectures and events. They hold a spring auction, a fall perennial and herb sale, summer garden tours and a seed swap. This asparagus is a fantastic spring dish.

Serves 4

2	pounds organic asparagus
4	tablespoons olive oil
4	cloves garlic, minced
1	teaspoon coarse sea salt

Freshly ground black pepper

2	lemons, cut into wedges

Preheat the oven to 450°F. Cut or snap off the bottom ½-inch of each asparagus spear. Arrange the spears on a baking sheet in a single layer. Sprinkle with oil, garlic, salt and pepper. Roll the spears to coat. Roast for 8 minutes, until crisp-tender. Serve with lemon wedges.

Courtesy of Front Range Organic Gardeners

VEGETARIAN ENTRÉES

Blue Corn Enchiladas with Goat Cheese

Blue corn tortillas and goat cheese give this dish a unique, but still traditional Southwestern texture and flavor.

Serves 4

6   tablespoons peanut or vegetable oil
½   cup thinly sliced onion
1   small red bell pepper, thinly sliced
½   green bell pepper, thinly sliced
8   blue corn tortillas
¼   pound Haystack Mountain goat cheese, or other goat cheese, crumbled
1   pound Monterey Jack cheese, shredded
Enchilada sauce (recipe follows)

Preheat the oven to 350°F. In a skillet, heat 2 tablespoons of the oil over medium heat and cook the onion and bell peppers until soft. Transfer to paper towels and drain. Add the remaining 4 tablespoons of oil to the skillet and cook the tortillas, one at a time, 5 seconds on each side. Drain on paper towels.

Fill the tortillas, first with vegetables, then with 1 tablespoon of crumbled goat cheese and 2 tablespoons shredded Monterey Jack cheese. Roll up the enchiladas and place them in a baking dish just large enough to hold 8 enchiladas. Spoon sauce over the enchiladas and sprinkle with the remaining Monterey Jack cheese. Bake until the cheese is melted and the enchiladas are heated through.

For the sauce:
2   tablespoons olive oil
½   white onion, minced
½   green bell pepper, minced
3   stalks celery, minced
4   cloves garlic, minced
3   cups canned crushed tomatoes
2   tablespoons ground cumin
1   teaspoon sugar
2   teaspoons paprika
1   teaspoon dried oregano
1   bay leaf
Cayenne pepper

In a heavy saucepan, heat the oil and cook the onions, bell pepper and celery over medium heat until soft. Add the garlic and cook for 1 minute. Add the tomatoes, cumin, sugar, paprika, oregano, bay leaf, salt and pepper. Add cayenne to taste. Simmer, covered, for 20 minutes. Discard bay leaf.

Courtesy of Haystack Mountain Goat Dairy

Cabbage Rolls

These are not traditional cabbage rolls – cabbage leaves wrapped around a filling. Instead, savory cabbage is enclosed in bread dough – a roll stuffed with cabbage.

Makes
6 to 8 rolls

½	large head cabbage, chopped
1	tablespoon vegetable oil
½	cup chopped onion
Pinch of paprika	
½	package yeast
¼	cup very warm water
1	cup milk
1	tablespoon honey
1	tablespoon butter
1	teaspoon salt
3	cups flour

Steam the cabbage in a little water until soft. In a large skillet, heat the oil and cook the onions until soft. Off the heat, add the paprika and stir to combine. Add the cabbage, stir to combine and set aside.

In a small bowl, sprinkle the yeast over the warm water. Wait 5 minutes for the yeast to soften, then stir to dissolve the yeast. Put the honey, butter and salt in a large bowl. Heat the milk just to boiling, then add it to the honey in the bowl. Mix until the butter is melted and combined. Add the yeast mixture and mix well. Add the flour and stir to form a stiff dough. Knead for 5 minutes, then shape into a ball. Cover and let rise until the dough doubles in volume.

Preheat the oven to 350°F. Punch the dough down and knead lightly. Roll the dough into a ¼-inch thick rectangle. Cut the dough into 2½-inch rounds. Place 3 to 5 tablespoons of the cabbage mixture into center of each dough round. Bring up the sides and pinch together. Place upside down on a greased cookie sheet. Cover with a damp towel and let rise for 10 to 15 minutes. Bake for 30 minutes, until golden brown. Serve immediately.

Courtesy of Eden Valley Farms

Pumpkins

It's the middle of October and you know what that means – pumpkins! At the market you'll find every variety from tiny to immense. Somewhere in the middle of the pumpkin 'spectrum' are the sugar pumpkins. These are smoother-looking and smaller than the typical jack-o-lantern pumpkins. They are heavy for their size because they have a thicker flesh wall and a smaller air space in the center. Sugar pumpkins have a sweet, fine-grained flesh for cooking and just enough seeds to roast for snacks.

If you've never cooked a pumpkin, you won't believe how easy it is. Pumpkins are part of the winter squash family, so you bake them just as you would any winter squash. First, wash the exterior and scrub lightly with a vegetable brush. Then, cut the pumpkin in half with a large, sharp knife. Scoop out the little bit of strings and seeds, saving the seeds for toasting. Discard the stem. Place the pumpkin halves cut side down on a greased baking sheet. Bake in a 325°F oven for about 45 minutes, or until you can easily pierce it with a knife. If the juice starts running out from the cut side, it's done. You want most of the juice to stay in the pumpkin. If you sample the small amount that does leak out, you will probably be surprised to find that it tastes sweet.

When the roasted pumpkin has cooled, simply scoop out the tender flesh. Mash it with a potato masher or process it in a food processor to make a purée (I find that it's a little too thick for the blender to handle). A small to mid-size sugar pumpkin will yield about three cups of cooked pumpkin. A typical 9-inch pie recipe requires two cups of purée.

Leftover pumpkin purée can be frozen. I usually freeze it in 2-cup portions, since that's the quantity called for in most recipes. This way it's easy to thaw and you just pour the purée into the mixing bowl. Not only is the purée perfect in pies; it is wonderful in muffins, quick breads, gingerbread and cookies. If you need more ideas, most general cookbooks include many recipes for using pumpkin.

bottom. Broil or grill the eggplant packages for 5 to 6 minutes, until browned on all sides.

To serve, place the lentils in a mound on each of 6 plates. Sprinkle with hazelnuts and top with an eggplant "package." Sprinkle chopped parsley on top and garnish with parsley sprigs.

Courtesy of The Fourth Story

Summer Vegetable Tian

Cook Street School of Fine Cooking specializes in the training of future culinary professionals through an intensive, accelerated Food and Wine Career Program. In addition, they offer a variety of enthusiast classes year-round for those who love to cook and enjoy the pleasures of the table. Stop by and visit the beautiful, European-inspired facility and experience a taste of Cook Street for yourself.

Serves 8

4	Japanese eggplants, cut into ¼-inch thick slices
4	medium zucchini, cut into ¼-inch slices
5	small to medium tomatoes, peeled and cut into ½-inch slices
4	cloves garlic, crushed
¼	cup extra virgin olive oil

Salt and black pepper
Fresh basil cut into thin strips (chiffanade) for garnish

Preheat the oven to 300°F. Toss separately the eggplant, zucchini and garlic with the olive oil. Season with salt and pepper.

In a round or square baking pan with 2-inch sides (a pie pan is fine), layer the sliced eggplant, zucchini and tomato in overlapping, alternating slices to tightly fit in the pan. Drizzle with a little olive oil and place in the oven.

Baste the vegetables with the liquid that accumulates in the bottom of the pan during baking. Bake the vegetables until they are very soft and the liquid in the bottom of the pan has almost evaporated. To serve, slice wedges or squares of the tian, drizzle with a little extra virgin olive oil and garnish with basil. The tian may be served hot or warm.

Courtesy of Cook Street School of Fine Cooking

Pumpkin Stuffed With Parmesan Risotto

The types of crops grown by The Fresh Herb Company change annually. "For example, next year you might not see tomatoes or eggplant. Perhaps we'd do more greens instead. They grow fast, everybody needs them and we can keep turning them over," says owner Chet Anderson. Anderson is always aware of what is "in" and adjusts his crop mix accordingly. Anderson doesn't just grow vegetables and herbs. Much of his crop is devoted to flowers, which he sells at the Boulder Farmers' Market and the Cherry Creek Fresh Market. This is a unique and impressive (but not impressively difficult) fall dinner.

Serves 4

2	small (1 to 1¼-pound) pie pumpkins
2	tablespoons butter or vegetable oil
1	cup chopped onion
1	cup Arborio rice
1	cup dried currants soaked in white wine for 10 minutes to plump (optional)
5-6	cups hot chicken or vegetable broth
1½	cups freshly grated Parmesan cheese

Salt and black pepper
2   cups balsamic vinegar
Green herbs to garnish, such as thyme and oregano

Preheat the oven to 425°F. Cut off the top of the pumpkins (like you would a jack-o'-lantern). Scoop out the seeds. Invert the pumpkins in a baking dish filled with a few inches of water. Bake the pumpkins until tender, but not mushy, about 20 to 30 minutes (the cooking time depends on the size of the pumpkins).

While the pumpkin is baking, put the vinegar in a small saucepan and boil it until it is the consistency of a syrup. Remove from the heat and cool.

Meanwhile, prepare the risotto. Heat the butter or oil in a large skillet. Add the onion and cook until soft, stirring occasionally. Add the rice and cook, stirring, until the rice is translucent. Add the currants and stir. Add the hot broth, 1 cup at a time, stirring often. As soon as each cup of broth is absorbed, add the next 1 cup and repeat until all of the broth has been absorbed. The rice is done when it is *al dente* and has a creamy texture, with most of the liquid absorbed. Add the cheese and mix thoroughly. Add salt and pepper to taste.

Place one-quarter of the balsamic syrup in the bottom of each pumpkin. Spoon the risotto into the pumpkin, mounding it at the top. Drizzle the remaining balsamic syrup over the risotto and garnish with a few sprigs of green herbs. To serve, cut the pumpkins in half. Eat the risotto and the pumpkin flesh.

Courtesy of The Fresh Herb Company

Goat Cheese and Leek Galette

Great goat cheese is the result of many elements, the most fundamental of which is the quality and taste of the milk. To achieve their "clean, sweet-tasting cheeses," Haystack Mountain's goats are fed a diet of dairy-quality alfalfa and mixed grains (oats, minerals and corn). This recipe, from Jason McHugh of Cooking School of the Rockies, makes a savory tart suitable for brunch or a light supper.

Serves
4 to 6

For the tart crust:

1	cup plus 2 tablespoons flour
¾	stick cold butter, cut into small pieces

Pinch of salt
Ice water as needed (approximately ¼ cup)

Put the flour, butter and salt in a food processor and pulse. Add 2 tablespoons of ice water and pulse several times. Check the consistency. If necessary, add more water, a little at a time, until the dough holds together. Wrap the dough in plastic wrap and refrigerate for at least 30 minutes.

For the galette filling:

3	leeks, white part cleaned and sliced, green part trimmed and reserved
2	tablespoons butter
2	bay leaves
8	ounces Haystack Mountain Spreadable Goat Cheese or ricotta cheese
1	teaspoon ground coriander
1	tablespoon chopped fresh thyme

Salt and white pepper

Melt the butter in a large saucepan over low heat. Add the leeks, cover and cook for 5 minutes. Add the bay leaf; cover and cook for 20 minutes, until the leeks are soft. Remove the leeks from the pan and cool slightly. Remove the bay leaf. Add the cheese, coriander and thyme; mix well. Season with salt and white pepper.

Roll out the tart dough on a floured surface until it is quite thin. Put the leek mixture in the center of the dough and flatten slightly. Enclose the leek and cheese mixture in the dough starting on one side and working around the dough clockwise. The leek and cheese mixture should be visible in the center of the dough. Chill the galette for 30 minutes.

Preheat the oven to 350°F. Place the galette on a baking sheet and bake for 35 to 45 minutes, until the crust is browned. Remove from the oven and cool slightly. To serve, slice the galette into wedges.

Courtesy of Haystack Mountain Goat Dairy

Bingham Hill Cheese and Fresh Vegetable Pizzas

Tom and Kristi Johnson spent their pre-cheese life trying to figure out why nobody in the region was making small-batch, artisanal cheese. They took up the challenge and have since been recognized as one of America's best producers of exquisite, small-batch cheeses. Here are some ideas for healthy and fresh pizzas made almost entirely from farmers' market ingredients. See what is in season and let your imagination go wild all summer and fall.

Tuscan Pizza

Fresh and Simple cheese is a creamy, spreadable cheese that puffs up a bit on this pizza and doesn't run off the sides. Try adding grilled chicken or some greens to it. Be sure to blanch the greens and squeeze out the water before adding them to the pizza, or you will get puddles.

Serves 4

4 ounces Bingham Hill Tuscan Herb Fresh & Simple cheese
Sally's pizza crust (recipe follows)
1 small red onion, halved vertically and sliced into half-moon-shaped slices
1 cup pitted kalamata olives
1 green, red and/or yellow bell pepper, sliced in rings
1 cup peeled and chopped tomatoes, preferably plum tomatoes

Preheat the oven to 450°F. Spread the cheese on the crust, then arrange the onion, olives, bell pepper and tomatoes on the cheese. Bake for 12 to 15 minutes.

Rustic Blue Pizza

This is a Bingham Hill staff favorite – even for those who scoff at having nuts on a pizza. Try it, you'll like it.

Serves 4

4 cups packed fresh spinach
1 Sally's pizza crust (recipe follows)
Walnut oil to brush on the crust (olive oil is also good)
2 cloves garlic, minced
4 Roma tomatoes, peeled and sliced (lengthwise looks good)
1 small (fist-sized) sweet yellow onion, chopped
¾ cup chopped walnuts
4 ounces Bingham Hill Rustic Blue Cheese, crumbled

Preheat the oven to 450°F. Blanch the spinach for 2 minutes in boiling water. Drain the spinach, cool it and then squeeze it to get rid of excess water. Chop the spinach and set aside.

Brush the pizza crust with oil and sprinkle with the garlic. Arrange the tomato slices on the crust, followed by the onion and the walnuts. Sprinkle with blue cheese and then top with the chopped spinach. Bake for 12 to 15 minutes.

Harvest Moon Pizza

Bingham Hill's Harvest Moon is made from raw cow's milk and has a beautiful orange rind. "It looks like the Fall moon rising from the plains," says Kristi Johnson. It is decidedly tart, similar to a very sharp East Coast cheddar.

Serves 4

20	thin stalks asparagus
1	Sally's pizza crust (recipe follows)
Olive oil for brushing on the crust	
2	cloves garlic, minced
10	green onions, chopped, including green tops
1	cup chopped ham, chicken or tofu
6	ounces grated Bingham Hill Harvest Moon cheese

Preheat the oven to 450°F. Steam the asparagus until crisp-tender, then put in ice water to stop the cooking process. Drain the asparagus, then cut it into 1-inch pieces. Brush the crust with olive oil and sprinkle with the garlic. Sprinkle the green onion, the tomatoes, the meat and then the asparagus over the pizza. Finally, sprinkle the cheese over it. Bake for 12 to 15 minutes.

For Sally's pizza crust:

Serves 4

1	package yeast
1	tablespoon sugar
1	cup very warm water
1	tablespoon olive oil
1	teaspoon salt
3-4	cups flour

Mix the yeast, sugar and very warm water in a large bowl; let the mixture sit until it is bubbly. Add the olive oil, salt and 3 cups of flour. Mix and knead to make a ball of soft dough (add more flour if it seems sticky). Put the dough in a greased glass bowl and put in a warm place to rise for about 45 minutes. Flatten the dough onto a pizza pan or pizza stone and let rise for another 30 minutes before using it.

Courtesy of Bingham Hill Cheese Company

Pasta with Sun-Cooked Sauce

Chris Burke was a city boy, born and raised in Chicago. He never guessed that he was destined to become a farmer. His passion for farming developed while he was attending college in Washington, where he worked on the school's organic farm. After school, Burke moved to Boulder, where he co-founded an organic fertilizer company. He started Burke Organic Farms in 1990 to test his fertilizers, and the farm gradually became his focus. This sauce is a Burke family favorite. It tastes best in summer, marinated in the sun or in a sunny window like Sun Tea.

Serves
4 to 6

2	pounds ripe Burke organic tomatoes, peeled and halved
½	cup chopped Burke organic basil
½	cup finely chopped red onion
2	tablespoons minced fresh parsley
2	tablespoons olive oil
¼	teaspoon salt
¼	teaspoon black pepper
1	pound favorite pasta, cooked according to package directions

Gently squeeze the tomatoes to extract the seeds, then chop them into ½-inch pieces. In a large bowl, combine the tomatoes, basil, red onion, parsley, olive oil, salt and pepper. Stir just to combine. Cover the bowl with a single layer of cheese-cloth and place outdoors in the sun or in a sunny window. Marinate for 4 to 5 hours. Toss the sauce with cooked pasta and serve.

Courtesy of Burke Organic Farms

Pasta and Market Vegetables with Orange Vinaigrette

Serves 4

1   ear fresh corn, grilled in the husk, kernels cut off the cob
2   red bell peppers, roasted, peeled, seeded and cut into thin strips
2   tablespoons finely chopped red onion
1   tomato, peeled and chopped
2   tablespoons finely chopped marjoram
2   tablespoons finely chopped basil
1   pound fresh linguini, or other fresh pasta
Orange vinaigrette (recipe follows)

Toss the corn, peppers, onion, tomato, marjoram and basil together in a bowl. Taste, then season with salt and pepper; set aside. Cook the pasta; drain and toss with the vegetables. Pour the vinaigrette over the warm pasta. Toss lightly and serve.

For the orange vinaigrette:
1   teaspoon ground cumin
zest and juice of 1 orange
3   tablespoons chopped fennel
3   tablespoons extra virgin olive oil
Salt and white pepper

Combine the cumin, orange juice, orange zest, fennel and oil. Let sit for about 20 minutes, then season to taste with salt and white pepper. Whisk before using.

Courtesy of Potager

Fresh Collard Greens with Pasta

If you haven't discovered collard greens already, this is a good way to introduce them to your family. After sampling this dish, even finicky eaters will agree that collard greens are as tasty as they are healthy.

Serves 4

1   pound collard greens
Balsamic vinegar to taste
½   stick butter
2   tablespoons pine nuts
2   cloves garlic, minced
2   ounces oil-packed sun-dried tomatoes, drained and cut into thin strips
Black or red pepper
1   pound cooked pasta (small shells or tri-color spirals work well)
Grated Parmesan cheese

Clean and stem the collard greens, removing tough ribs. Cut the leaves into ½-inch strips. Wash the leaves, but do not dry them.

In a large skillet with enough water to just cover the bottom of the pan, add the damp collard greens (depending on how large the skillet is, this may have to be done in 2 to 3 batches). Splash vinegar over the top of the greens. Bring to a boil, cover and cook for 2 minutes, then uncover and toss until all of the leaves turn bright green. At this point, the greens will be crisp-tender – continue to cook the greens until they begin to turn an olive color. Remove from the heat.

Melt the butter in a large skillet over medium heat. Add the pine nuts and garlic; cook until the garlic begins to brown (be careful not to burn it). Add the sun-dried tomatoes and pepper; cook until the sun-dried tomatoes are heated through. Add the collard greens; cover and cook until the greens are heated through, about 1 minute. Add the pasta and toss. Adjust the seasonings and serve with Parmesan cheese.

Courtesy of Grant Family Farms

MEAT, POULTRY, GAME & FISH

Colorado Potato Lasagna

Most of Colorado's potato crop is grown in the San Luis Valley, a very fertile, high alpine basin in south-central Colorado. The valley is nestled between the majestic mountains of the Sangre de Cristo and the San Juan ranges. Local farmers began growing potatoes in the Valley in the late 19th century, making it one of the oldest potato growing areas in the country.

Serves 6

1	pound ground beef
½	cup chopped onion
1½	cups sliced mushrooms
1	large clove garlic, minced
2	cups marinara sauce
2	tablespoons chopped parsley
6	cups thinly sliced potatoes (about 4 medium potatoes), peeled if desired
½	cup grated mozzarella cheese
2	tablespoons grated Parmesan cheese

In a non-stick skillet over medium heat, brown the beef. Drain off any fat. Add the onions, mushrooms and garlic. Cook until the onions are tender and the mushrooms are golden. Stir in the marinara sauce and parsley; heat through.

Preheat the oven to 375°F. In a greased, 9x13-inch baking dish, arrange half the potato slices. Top with half the meat sauce. Top with the remaining potatoes and then the remaining meat sauce. Cover tightly with foil and bake for 50 to 60 minutes, until the potatoes are tender. Uncover, sprinkle with the cheeses and bake for 5 minutes more. Let stand for 5 minutes before serving.

Courtesy of Colorado Potato Administrative Committee

Chile Relleno Bake

Grassmick Produce and Coin operates a market at their farm, located two miles west of Rocky Ford, in southern Colorado. Asparagus is the first crop to arrive, in mid-April. Local schools sell flowers from the Grassmick greenhouse each year as a fundraiser. Sweet corn is the farm's main crop, along with squash, cucumbers, tomatoes and peppers. The farm offers homemade jellies from their orchard, as well as their unique spicy tomato jelly. In the off-season, the farm runs coin shows around the country, thus "Grassmick Produce and Coin."

Serves
8 to 10

1	pound ground beef or bulk pork, turkey or chicken sausage
½	cup chopped onion
10	mild chiles, roasted, seeded and peeled (or 10 canned, whole chiles)
1	teaspoon salt
¼	teaspoon black pepper
4	eggs, beaten
¼	cup flour
1½	cups milk
6	ounces cheddar cheese, grated

Brown the ground beef and onion in a skillet. Drain the fat. Remove from the heat and add ½ teaspoon of salt and the pepper.

Preheat the oven to 350°F. Place half of the chiles in the bottom of a greased 8x8-inch baking dish. Top with the meat. Arrange the rest of the chiles on top.

Combine the eggs, flour, ½ teaspoon of salt and milk. Mix until smooth. Pour over the chiles. Top with cheese. Bake for 45 minutes.

Courtesy of Grassmick Produce & Coin

Beef and Couscous-Stuffed Roasted Peppers

This recipe brings a Mediterranean twist to traditional stuffed peppers. Couscous is used instead of rice and the olives and feta cheese add a Greek flavor.

Serves 6

4	large red or yellow bell peppers (7 to 9 ounces each)
1	pound 80% lean ground beef
1	cup chopped zucchini
¼	teaspoon salt
¼	teaspoon black pepper
1¼	cups water
1	6-ounce package olive oil and garlic-flavored couscous mix
2	tablespoons coarsely chopped pitted kalamata olives
½	cup crumbled feta cheese.

Preheat the oven to 450°F. Halve the peppers vertically, then seed them. Place the peppers, cut-side down, in a baking dish. Bake for 10 to 15 minutes, or until the pepper skins begin to brown. Remove from the oven and set aside.

While the peppers are roasting, cook the ground beef and zucchini in a large, non-stick skillet, over medium heat, breaking up the beef into ½-inch crumbles. Cook for 8 to 10 minutes, or until the beef is no longer pink. Drain any fat and season with salt and pepper.

Stir the water and the seasoning packet from the couscous mix into the ground beef. Bring to a boil. Stir in the couscous and feta cheese. Remove from the heat, cover and let stand for 5 minutes to cook the couscous, then stir in the olives.

Stuff one-quarter of the beef mixture into each roasted pepper half. Bake until the beef mixture is heated through and the cheese is melted, about 5 minutes.

Courtesy of the Colorado Beef Council

Blue Cheese-Stuffed Burgers

In 1979, Mel Coleman, a fourth generation Colorado rancher and the company's founder, pioneered the marketing of pure and natural beef raised humanely and with respect for the environment. Today, Coleman Natural Products is the leading American supplier of fresh, natural beef from cattle that have never received added hormones or antibiotics. These burgers are very juicy and are always a hit. Use any blue cheese that you like, such as Bingham Hill from Fort Collins. The burgers can be made ahead and frozen, then thawed before cooking.

Serves 4

1   pound Coleman Natural ground chuck, or other ground beef
Salt and black pepper
2   teaspoons Worcestershire or steak sauce
1   cup crumbled blue cheese
1   tablespoon butter, at room temperature
½   cup finely chopped green onion

In a large bowl, combine the ground beef and Worcestershire sauce. Season with salt and pepper. Form the mixture into 8 equal patties about ⅜-inch thick. Cover the patties and put them in the refrigerator while you prepare the stuffing.

Put the cheese and butter in a small bowl and blend with a fork. Add the onions and stir until the mixture is creamy.

Remove the patties from the refrigerator. Place an equal amount of the cheese mixture in the center of each of 4 burger patties. Cover the stuffing with the remaining 4 burger patties and seal the edges by pressing them together with your fingers. Grill, broil or pan fry the burgers until done to your taste.

Courtesy of Coleman Natural Products

Cooking That Great Steak

The one thing many of the country's leading fine restaurant chefs know is how to cook a great-tasting, tender, juicy steak. The tools of the trade – broilers, pans and grills – are found in almost every home. Simply knowing how to use these tools can make a steak great. Broiling a steak at home is not recommended because most broilers in conventional ovens do not reach the extreme temperatures (up to 800°F) that broilers in professional kitchens do. These extreme temperatures make the great restaurant steak – seared on the outside, juicy on the inside.

When cooking a steak, preheat the grill or skillet to a very high heat. To determine how hot the grill is, hold your hand about four inches above the heat. If you pull your hand away in two seconds, it's extremely hot. If you pull away in five seconds, the temperature is considered low. Cook the steak for one to two minutes on each side over extreme temperatures so that the meat sears, locking in its natural juices. Once the steak is seared, lower the heat a little to ensure proper, even cooking throughout the rest of the cut. To preserve the steak's natural tenderness, be sure not to overcook it.

Determining how long to cook a steak depends not only on the cooking temperature, but also on how thick the cut is. Naturally, the thicker the cut, the longer the cooking time. Most steaks are cooked by direct heat, where the heat source is directly under the steak, such as on a grill or in a ridged cast iron skillet. Direct heat is best for steaks graded prime or choice, because the marbling makes the steak cook faster. Another method, using indirect heat, where the heat source is not directly underneath the steak, will help leaner steaks, or those graded select, become more tender.

Professional chefs usually test doneness by pushing the meat with their fingers to determine how firm it is. The firmer the steak, the more done it is. It's important to remember that thicker steaks continue cooking off the heat. By taking the steak off the heat a minute or two before you think it's done and letting it sit for five to ten minutes minutes, it will cook to perfection. Another tip from the chefs is to always use tongs or a metal spatula to turn a steak. Never use a fork, because puncturing the meat allows its natural juices to escape.

Courtesy of Coleman Natural Products

Red, White and Blue Steak

The (red) steak, (white) onion and (blue) cheese make a festive summer entrée. Serve this patriotic steak over rice, potatoes or polenta.

Serves 4

1½ pounds porterhouse steak
Sea salt and black pepper
Minced garlic to taste
Fresh oregano and/or thyme leaves
1 Colorado sweet onion, sliced ⅜-inch thick
Olive oil
Balsamic vinegar
Bingham Hill Rustic Blue Cheese, or other blue cheese, crumbled

Season the steak with salt, pepper and garlic to taste; cover and set aside for at least 15 minutes. Preheat the grill – one side on high, the other side low. Put the onion on a plate. Drizzle it with the olive oil and balsamic vinegar, then sprinkle it with salt and pepper.

Grill the onion on the low heat portion of the grill (or on the edge if using a charcoal grill), slowly cooking it until tender. Grill the steak on the hot side of the grill (or directly over the coals) for 5 to 7 minutes.

Turn the steak, lower the heat to medium (or move to the edge of the coals) and sprinkle generously with the blue cheese. Cover the grill and continue to cook the steak until it is done to your taste (about 5 minutes longer for rare).

Remove the steak to a plate, sprinkle with fresh herbs and tent with foil, allowing it to rest for at least 5 minutes. Slice the steak and arrange the slices on a plate with the grilled onions. Drizzle the steak and onions to taste with balsamic vinegar, then sprinkle with more cheese, if desired.

Courtesy of Chef Mick Rosacci, Tony's Meats & Specialty Foods

Southwestern Chipotle Sirloin Steak

Maverick Ranch products combine Old West, natural livestock raising methods with state-of-the-art technology. The result is great tasting natural beef that melts in your mouth. In 1987, Maverick Ranch became a supplier to the U.S. Olympic Training Centers. Since then, the ranch has donated all of the beef to feed 18,000 to 20,000 athletes at the centers each year. As a result, Maverick Ranch Beef has truly become "the beef behind the U.S. Olympic athletes." Instead of the usual steak on the grill, try marinating your meat with this Southwestern rub. The rub's flavor pairs perfectly with a fresh salsa made from your other farmers' market purchases. Serve the steaks with rice and beans or enchiladas. Chipotle chiles are available dried or canned in the Mexican food section of most groceries.

Serves 4

1	tablespoon minced chipotle chile
1	tablespoon ground cumin
1	tablespoon chili powder
3	tablespoons paprika
1	tablespoon brown sugar
1	tablespoon garlic powder
1	tablespoon kosher salt
1	tablespoon black pepper
4	10-ounce Maverick Ranch top sirloin steaks
1	tablespoon olive oil

In a large mixing bowl, combine the chipotle chile, cumin, chili powder, paprika, brown sugar, garlic powder, salt and pepper. Dredge both side of the steaks in this seasoning mix. Lightly brush the steaks with canola oil, then grill to your desired doneness (Maverick Ranch suggests medium-rare).

Courtesy of Maverick Ranch

Brisket Birria

Princess Beef raises organic, grass-fed beef in Crawford, in southwestern Colorado. The Southwestern flavors in this brisket make it perfect to serve with warm tortillas, beans and rice. Allow plenty of time to cook the meat – the slow roasting allows the flavors to develop. This recipe can also be cooked in a crockpot.

Serves
4 to 6

¼ cup ground red chile powder
1½ cups dry red wine
¼ cup red wine vinegar
6 cloves garlic, crushed
1½ teaspoons ground cumin
1½ teaspoons dried oregano
½ teaspoon cinnamon
1 (3 to 5 pound) Princess brisket or chuck roast
4 onions, thinly sliced

Preheat the oven to 250°F. In a small bowl, mix the chile powder, wine, vinegar, garlic, cumin, oregano and cinnamon. Place the brisket in a greased roasting pan. Pour the wine mixture over the brisket and top with the onions. Cover tightly with foil or the lid of the roasting pan (or crockpot). Bake for 6 hours (or cook in a crock pot at the low setting), until the meat is so tender that it falls apart. Shred with a fork to serve.

Courtesy of Princess Beef

Meatloaf in a Potato Blanket

Meatloaf is one of those wonderful comfort foods. And when you wrap it in mashed potatoes, all your troubles melt away.

Serves
10 to 12

1½ pounds ground beef
½ cup soft bread crumbs
⅓ cup minced onion
1 egg, beaten
½ cup ketchup
1¼ teaspoons salt
½ teaspoon black pepper
3 cups cooked, mashed Colorado potatoes
¼ cup minced green onion
3 tablespoons chopped parsley
Fresh chives for garnish

Preheat the oven to 350°F. In a large bowl, combine the beef, bread crumbs, onion, egg, ketchup, 1 teaspoon salt and ⅛ teaspoon pepper. Blend well and shape into a 4x8-inch loaf. Place in a shallow baking pan and bake for 75 minutes.

Meanwhile, combine the potatoes, green onion, parsley, ¼ teaspoon salt and ⅛ teaspoon pepper. After the meatloaf has baked for 75 minutes, remove it from the oven and spread the mashed potatoes over the top and sides of the loaf. Bake the loaf for 20 more minutes. If desired, broil until golden. Garnish with fresh chives.

Courtesy of the Colorado Potato Administrative Committee

RIPE

Bob Castellino (top left); Paul Bousquet (top right, bottom left, bottom right)

BEETS

GOLD

SANGRE RED POTATOES

MARKET FRESH

JUICY

Paul Bousquet (top left and bottom); Rich Abrahamson (top right)

EARLY
BIRD

COUNTY
RMERS
ARKET

ONESDAY 10-2
TURDAY 8-2

GARDEN

Paul Bousquet (top and bottom); Mark Fox (middle);

FRESH

ORCHARD

Bob Castellino (top); Rich Abrahamson (middle); Paul Bousquet (bottom)

Goat Cheese-Stuffed Chicken Breasts with Salsa Verde

This recipe was created by Jason McHugh at Cooking School of the Rockies. Note: the salsa verde needs to be made at least several hours ahead for the flavors to combine.

Serves 4

4	boneless, skinless chicken breasts
½	cup crumbled Haystack Mountain Smoked Chèvre
½	cup crumbled Haystack Mountain goat ricotta
2	red bell peppers, roasted, peeled and minced
4	scallions, minced

Olive oil
Salt and black pepper
Salsa verde (recipe follows)

Preheat the oven to 350°F. Lightly pound the chicken breasts at the thickest part. Combine the cheeses, red pepper and scallions. Season with salt and pepper; mix well.

Stuff each chicken breast with one-quarter of the cheese mixture. Roll up each breast, folding in the excess meat around the cheese. Lightly grease a baking sheet and place the breasts, seam side down, on the pan. Brush with oil and season with salt and pepper. Bake for 20 to 30 minutes, or until cooked through. Slice thinly on the bias and serve with salsa verde.

For the salsa verde:

6	cloves garlic, minced
½	cup chopped, stemmed fresh parsley
3	tablespoons chopped fresh basil
1	tablespoon chopped tarragon
2	tablespoons capers, chopped
½	cup extra virgin olive oil

Salt and black pepper
2-3 anchovies, minced (optional)

Mix all of the ingredients together and let sit, covered and refrigerated, for several hours or overnight to combine the flavors.

Courtesy of Haystack Mountain Goat Dairy

Easy Buffalo Cooking Tips

Substitute buffalo (American bison) for beef – it's perfectly okay! You can make burgers, steaks, roasts, tacos, meatloaf, chili, stew, ribs, enchiladas, kabobs, the list goes on...

Because ground buffalo is leaner than ground beef, it cooks faster, so be careful not to overcook it. For burgers, try cooking the meat further from the heat source. Lower the temperature a bit and please, "when you flip 'em, don't squish 'em!" (When you press down on the patties with a spatula, you push out all the juices into the coals.)

Burgers are done when they are cooked to medium and not more than medium-well. In general, the thicker the burgers, the juicier they will be. One-third pound burgers are about perfect. They are thick and juicy, yet not so big that they end up under- or overcooked.

Buffalo steaks are also leaner than their beef counterparts. For the best flavor, cook them to rare or medium. The guidelines are follows:

1-inch steaks:	6 to 8 minutes for rare; 10 to 12 minutes for medium
1½-inch steaks:	10 to 12 minutes for rare; 14 to 18 minutes for medium

Bison roasts are best cooked slowly in the crockpot all day on the low temperature setting, or roasted in the oven at 200°F to 225°F for 6 to 8 hours (using a meat thermometer will help you know when the roast has finished cooking). Either way, you will want to add some type of liquid to the roast. Try using soup, broth, salsa or water mixed with your favorite spices (you can season bison roasts like beef). Baste the roast occasionally during the cooking time.

Courtesy of Buffalo Groves, Inc.

Buffalo Tenderloin with Cranberry Chipotle Sauce

New West Foods, formerly the Denver Buffalo Company (DBC), has been the leading marketing company of buffalo (American bison) products since 1990. New West Foods still offers the best DBC-branded buffalo products, but they are now the one-stop shop to find all of your all-natural specialty meats – from alligator, venison, ostrich and wild boar, to elk and more. This is a good recipe to serve when you have out-of-state company for dinner. It is elegant, flavorful and very Western. The sweet-tart flavor of cranberries combined with the spice of chipotle chiles brings out the flavor of buffalo. Buffalo tenderloins are available at many natural and specialty food markets. Chipotle peppers are available dried or canned in the Mexican food section of most groceries.

Serves 12

1   (5 to 7 pound) buffalo tenderloin
Salt and black pepper
1   pound applewood smoked bacon
Cranberry chipotle sauce (recipe follows)

Preheat the oven to 425°F. Rinse the tenderloin under cool tap water and pat dry. Lightly season with salt and pepper. Wrap the meat with bacon, securing with toothpicks. Put the tenderloin in a roasting pan and roast in the oven until a meat thermometer reads 130°F for medium rare (about 20 minutes per pound), 140°F for medium (35 to 40 minutes per pound).

For the cranberry chipotle sauce:
4   chipotle peppers, chopped
1   small onion, chopped
1   red bell pepper, chopped
1   12-ounce bottle dark beer
2   cloves garlic, minced
1   cup packed brown sugar
1½   cups cider vinegar
½   cup tomato paste
¼   cup dark molasses
4   cups whole cranberries, fresh or frozen

Combine all of the sauce ingredients in a saucepan. Simmer, uncovered, for 20 minutes. Cool slightly, then purée in a blender or food processor. Reheat the sauce and serve it over the tenderloin.

Courtesy of New West Foods

Moist Buffaloaf

Buffalo Groves specializes in gourmet, grass-fed buffalo meat (bison), raised with no additives, antibiotics, preservatives, growth hormones or grain – nothing but grass. Buffalo Groves will ship overnight to nearly anywhere. They also carry buffalo head mounts, buffalo robes, buffalo skulls, and a fun assortment of unique bison gifts. This is an exceptional buffalo meatloaf with a delicious gravy made by topping the meatloaf with cream of mushroom soup before baking. The unused bell pepper halves and onion can be sliced, sautéed in olive oil until soft and served over the buffaloaf.

Serves 4

2 pounds ground bison
½ red bell pepper, chopped
½ yellow bell pepper, chopped
½ green bell pepper, chopped
½ large red onion, chopped
Garlic powder to taste
Salt and black pepper
¼ cup ketchup
2 tablespoons Worcestershire sauce
2 eggs, lightly beaten
1 cup breadcrumbs
1 10¾-ounce can condensed cream of mushroom soup

Preheat the oven to 375°F. In a large bowl, combine the buffalo, bell peppers, onion, garlic powder, salt and pepper, ketchup, Worcestershire and eggs. Add breadcrumbs as needed for the mixture to form a firm loaf. Place in a loaf pan.

In a medium saucepan, mix the mushroom soup with 1 soup can of water. Heat, stirring to combine well. Drizzle the soup over the meatloaf to within ¼-inch of the top of the pan. Reserve any remaining soup to use as extra gravy. Cover the pan with foil and bake until thoroughly cooked, about 1½ to 2 hours (until a meat thermometer inserted in the center of the loaf reaches 160°F). Serve in slices smothered with the gravy.

Courtesy of Buffalo Groves

Buffalo Pepper Steaks with Dijon Cream Sauce

In this recipe, buffalo steaks are dressed up with a Dijon cream sauce to create a gourmet entrée. Try grilling the steaks for even greater flavor. Buffalo steaks are available at many groceries and natural and specialty food markets.

Serves 4

2   16-ounce (¾-inch thick) buffalo top sirloin steaks
Garlic salt and black pepper
4   teaspoons black peppercorns, coarsely ground or crushed
5   tablespoons Dijon mustard
2   tablespoons olive or vegetable oil
½   cup minced shallots
1   clove garlic, minced
1   cup beef broth
¼   cup whipping cream
¼   cup brandy

Rinse the steaks under cool tap water and pat dry. Dust each side with garlic salt and coarse black pepper. Spread 2 tablespoons of mustard on one side of each steak. Sprinkle with 1 teaspoon peppercorns and press into the steaks. Turn and repeat the process for each steak.

Heat the oil in a skillet over high heat. Add the steaks and cook to your desired doneness, about 5 minutes on each side for medium-rare. When done, remove the steaks and keep warm. Do not drain or clean the skillet.

Add the shallots and garlic to the skillet used to cook the steak and cook for about 15 to 20 seconds. Stir in the broth, cream, brandy and 1 tablespoon of mustard. Bring to a boil and thicken, about 2 minutes. Serve the steaks topped with the Dijon cream sauce.

Courtesy of New West Foods

Brine-Cured Pork Chops

Brining yields impressively juicy and flavorful chops. The pork chops need to marinate in the salt, maple syrup and herb mixture for at least 24 hours.

Serves 2

½	cup maple syrup
¾	cup water
2	tablespoons salt
1	tablespoon yellow mustard seeds
1	rosemary sprig
1	thyme sprig
1	sage sprig
2	bay leaves
2	Maverick Ranch natural pork chops

Bring all of the ingredients, except the pork chops, to a boil in a saucepan. Cool completely and then pour over the pork chops. Marinate the chops for 24 to 36 hours, covered and refrigerated. Remove the meat from the brine and discard the brine. Grill the pork chops until done.

Courtesy of Potager

Honey Pepper Pork Roast

Serves 6

1	boneless pork roast (about 2½ pounds)
½	cup honey
2	tablespoons Dijon mustard
1½	teaspoons chopped fresh thyme, or ½ teaspoon dried thyme
1	tablespoon crushed mixed peppercorns
½	teaspoon salt

Honey cranberry relish (see recipe on page 11)

Preheat the oven to 325°F. Score the entire roast ¼-inch deep, taking care not to cut the string holding the roast together. Combine the honey, mustard, thyme, peppercorns and salt in a small bowl. Place the roast on a rack in a roasting pan. Spoon or brush two-thirds of the honey mixture over the pork to coat.

Bake the pork roast for 30 minutes; then brush the remaining honey mixture over the pork. Roast for 25 more minutes, or until a meat thermometer reaches 160-165°F. Let the roast stand for 10 minutes, tented with foil, before slicing. Serve with honey cranberry relish.

Courtesy of J&J Apiaries

Sausage Eggplant Parmesan

At the turn of the century, when many Italian immigrants were settling in Denver, Old World family recipes were treasured heirlooms – pieces of a family's heritage. When Joseph Canino married Lena Pagliano in 1917, Joseph's mother gave the couple her sausage recipe brought from Calabria, Italy. Thus, Canino's sausage was born. Family strength and determination, original recipes, natural casings, low fat content and natural ingredients have made Canino's Sausages a legacy Grandma Canino would be proud of.

Serves 4

12   (½-inch thick) slices peeled eggplant
2   pounds Canino's hot or mild Italian sausage
1   tablespoon olive oil
½   cup chopped onion
½   cup chopped green bell pepper
2   tablespoons flour
½   teaspoon oregano
2   cups tomato sauce (or pizza or spaghetti sauce)
2   cups grated mozzarella cheese
½   cup grated Parmesan cheese
Salt and black pepper

Cook the eggplant in boiling water until tender, about 5 minutes. Drain and set aside. Preheat the oven to 300°F. Brown the sausage; drain and set aside.

In a large skillet, heat the olive oil. Add the onion and green pepper; cook until tender. Add the sausage and stir in the flour and oregano. Season to taste with salt and pepper. Add the tomato sauce and cook until thickened.

Arrange half the eggplant slices in a shallow, 2-quart, greased baking dish. Top with half of the sausage mixture and then half of the cheese. Repeat the layers and bake, uncovered, for 30 minutes. Serve with extra Parmesan cheese.

Courtesy of Canino's Sausage

Roasted Loin of Colorado Lamb with Haystack Mountain Goat Cheese and Potato Custard and Thyme Merlot Sauce

Created by Chef Mark Black of Denver's Brown Palace Hotel, when he was guest chef at The James Beard House.

Serves 8

For the potato custard:

2   baking potatoes, chopped
2   tablespoons butter, melted
¾   teaspoon salt
Pinch of white pepper
4   ounces Haystack Mountain goat cheese
6   eggs
½   cup heavy cream
Pinch of freshly grated nutmeg
2   tablespoons chopped chives

Preheat the oven to 375°F. Place the potatoes in a plastic bag with the butter, salt and pepper; shake to coat. Roast the potatoes for 25 minutes, or until tender. When the potatoes are done, remove to a bowl.

Lower the oven temperature to 250°F. Crumble the cheese into the potatoes; stir to combine. Divide the potatoes among 8 greased 4-ounce soufflé dishes (or a 2-quart ceramic or glass baking dish). Combine the eggs, cream, nutmeg and chives; pour over the potatoes and bake for 40 minutes (or longer if using a baking dish).

For the lamb:

4   lamb loins, cleaned
Salt and black pepper

Season the lamb and sear in hot pans. Finish in a 325°F oven for 15 minutes, until done to your taste.

For the thyme merlot sauce:

¼   teaspoon minced garlic
1   teaspoon minced shallots
1   tablespoon butter
¾   cup Merlot wine
2½ cups lamb broth (or beef broth)
1   teaspoon chopped thyme
1   bay leaf
Salt and white pepper

Cook the garlic and shallots in the butter until translucent. Add the wine and reduce by half. Add the broth, thyme and bay leaf and reduce by half. Strain the sauce and season to taste with salt and white pepper. Serve the lamb with the thyme Merlot sauce, accompanied by the potato custard.

Courtesy of Haystack Mountain Goat Dairy

Braised Colorado Lamb Shanks

This is a most requested recipe – several guests at a recipe testing dinner called later asking for it.

Serves 4

2	Colorado lamb shanks, split
Sea salt and black pepper	
2	teaspoons mixed dried herbs, such as rosemary, basil, thyme, etc.
Flour	
2	tablespoons vegetable oil
1	cup minced carrot
1	cup minced onion
½	cup minced celery
1	large clove garlic, minced
1	cup beef broth
¾	cup red wine
Sprig of oregano	
Sprig of thyme	
1	bay leaf
1	tablespoon tomato paste

Preheat the oven to 275°F. Season the shanks with sea salt, pepper and assorted herbs, then toss in flour to coat well.

Heat a heavy pot. Add the oil and lamb shanks; brown on all sides. Remove to an oven-proof baking dish. Add the vegetables and garlic to the browning pot and cook for 5 minutes, or until soft. Add the wine, broth, tomato paste, oregano, thyme and bay leaf. Bring to a boil and pour over the lamb. Cover with a tight-fitting lid and roast for 2½ hours, turning once and adding water if needed.

Skim and serve the shanks with the pan sauce as is, or purée the vegetables in the cooking liquid for a thicker sauce.

Courtesy of Chef Mick Rosacci, Tony's Meats & Specialty Foods

Green Chile Lamb Roast

Wholesome Harvest Farm raises natural lamb, chicken, eggs, fruits and vegetables. The farm is located north of Ignacio, in southern Colorado.

Serves 14

1	(3 to 5 pound) boneless, rolled lamb roast, trimmed
1	teaspoon oregano
1	teaspoon dried sage
½	teaspoon black pepper
1	tablespoon olive oil
2	medium onions, chopped
2	cloves garlic, minced
1	14-ounce can chopped tomatoes, undrained
½	cup chopped roasted green chiles
½	cup water
¼	cup vinegar
1	tablespoon chili powder
1	teaspoon salt

Preheat the oven to 325°F. Place the lamb on a rack in a shallow baking pan. Combine the oregano, sage and pepper; rub over the lamb. Roast the lamb, uncovered, for 35 to 40 minutes per pound, until cooked to desired doneness. Cover the roast with foil and let stand for 15 minutes before carving.

Meanwhile, heat the olive oil in a saucepan over medium heat. Cook the onion and garlic, stirring occasionally, until the onions are tender. Add the undrained tomatoes, chiles, water, vinegar, chili powder and salt. Bring to a boil. Reduce the heat to low and simmer, uncovered, for 20 minutes. Remove from the heat. Baste the lamb with this mixture during the last hour of roasting time.

Courtesy of Wholesome Harvest Farm

Jalapeño-Glazed Elk Tenderloin

Colorado Elk and Game Meats is located at 7,000 feet in the heart of the San Juan mountains. Comprised of three ranches, Colorado Elk and Game operates on nearly 1,000 acres of mountain pastures cultivated with native grasses and alfalfa. Spacious meadows are filled with majestic Rocky Mountain Elk. Elk is naturally low in fat and cholesterol, yielding healthy, gourmet fare suitable for the best white tablecloth entrées, such as this elk tenderloin.

Serves
4 to 6

1½	cups Burgundy wine
1½	teaspoons ground ginger
2	tablespoons chile caribe (crushed red chile flakes)
1	(2 to 4 pound) elk tenderloin (or pork or beef tenderloin)
3	cloves garlic, slivered
¼	cup chopped onion
½	cup jalapeño jelly
6	thick slices bacon

Combine the wine, ginger and chile caribe; set aside. With a sharp knife, carefully pierce the elk about 1-inch deep all over. Insert a sliver of garlic in each slit. Set the roast in an oven-proof, glass roasting dish and top with the onion. Drizzle the wine mixture over the tenderloin. Let stand at room temperature for at least 2 hours (and up to 6 to 8 hours, if time permits), basting frequently.

Preheat the oven to 450°F. Drain the marinade and reserve for basting. Glaze the meat with the jelly, spooning and smoothing uniformly over all sides. Wrap the bacon around the roast, laying the slices next to one another. Fasten the bacon with skewers or tie it with cooking twine. Roast the meat for 15 minutes, or until the bacon begins to crisp. Lower the oven temperature to 325°F and roast until cooked to desired doneness, basting after 15 minutes with the reserved marinade for a 2 pound roast, and again after 30 minutes for a 4 pound roast. Allow about 10 minutes per pound for rare. Check for doneness with a meat thermometer – the desired doneness is rare (115°F) to medium (130°F).

When the meat is done roasting, let it stand for at least 30 minutes to let the juices set. Carve the meat across the grain into ¼- to ½-inch thick slices, cutting through the bacon so each slice of tenderloin is encircled with bacon.

Courtesy of Colorado Elk and Game Meats

Hazelnut Crusted Roasted Venison Loin with Sweet Potato Purée and Cranberry Orange Compote

La Tour Restaurant, located in the Vail Village, features light, contemporary French cuisine utilizing the highest quality products. The menu changes with the seasons and always features exciting dishes. Chef and owner Paul Ferzacca says of his cooking "Simplicity is the mother of beauty." This exceptional venison dish needs only a salad or a green vegetable (or both) to make a gourmet meal. Even better, you can make the sauce base, the compote and the sweet potatoes up to two days in advance. If venison is not available, you can substitute beef tenderloin.

Serves 6

1   pound whole cranberries, fresh or frozen
1   cup freshly squeezed orange juice
1   cup sugar
3   cinnamon sticks
2   sticks unsalted butter plus 2 tablespoons salted butter
1   cup plus ½ cup heavy cream
2   teaspoons minced fresh sage
2   tablespoons plus 1 cup toasted, finely ground skinless hazelnuts
3–4 large sweet potatoes
Salt and white pepper
2½ pounds venison short loin (or beef tenderloin)
Ground cinnamon
2   tablespoons Canola oil plus more for coating meat

To make the compote, put the cranberries, orange juice, sugar and cinnamon sticks in a large saucepan over high heat, stirring to mix well. Bring to a boil, then lower the heat to medium-high. When the cranberries begin to crack, remove the pan from the heat and let cool. Keep refrigerated until ready to serve (up to 1 month). The compote may be served hot or cold.

For the sauce, put the 2 sticks of unsalted butter and 1 cup of cream in a medium saucepan over high heat. Stir often. When the mixture begins to boil, lower the heat. Keep the mixture gently boiling until it starts to brown and separate, about 25 to 30 minutes. Whisk the sauce to break up the brown milk solids and remove from the heat. At this point, you can cool the sauce and refrigerate it until you are ready to use it (up to 1 week). When you are ready to use the sauce, warm it over very low heat, then whisk in the sage and the 2 tablespoons of hazelnuts.

For the sweet potatoes, preheat the oven to 350°F. Prick the sweet potatoes with a knife in several places and put directly on the oven rack. Roast until tender, about 20 minutes. Before you remove the potatoes from the oven, put the 2 tablespoons of salted butter and ½ cup of cream in a small saucepan. Heat until the butter is melted and the mixture is warm. Remove the potatoes from the oven, cut in half and scoop the pulp into a large bowl. Add the warm cream mixture to the potatoes and mash until all of the liquid is incorporated and the potatoes are smooth. Season with salt and white pepper. If you are not serving right away, cool, then store in airtight container in the refrigerator for up to 2 days. Reheat when ready to serve. If the potatoes seem dry, mix in a little melted butter and/or cream.

For the meat, preheat the oven to 350°F. Cut the meat into 6 equal portions and brush on both sides with oil. Season with salt, pepper and cinnamon. Cover both sides of meat with hazelnuts. In a large, oven-proof skillet, heat the 2 tablespoons of oil. Add the meat and brown on both sides over medium-high heat. Transfer the skillet to the oven and roast until the meat is done to your taste (10 to 15 minutes for rare). Remove from the oven and let sit while you assemble the plates.

To serve: Place a mound of sweet potato purée on each of 6 warm plates. Spoon a little sauce next to the sweet potatoes and place the meat in the middle of the sauce. Put a large dollop of the compote next to the meat, then drizzle a little more sauce over the meat and potatoes. Serve immediately, passing extra sauce and compote.

Courtesy of La Tour Restaurant

Chile Crusted Red Trout on Cornbread and Chard with Market Succotash

The menu at Q's, in Boulder, changes monthly to take advantage of the freshest seasonal ingredients. Chef and owner John Platt has a talent for creating unique and interesting combinations with complementary textures and tastes, such as this combination of Southwestern flavors, fresh fish and seasonal vegetables.

Serves 6

6	6-ounce fillets red trout (or the delicious Copper River salmon when it's available in early summer), skin on
	Olive oil
	Salt and black pepper
	Ground cumin
	Ground red chile (not chili powder)
4	ounces applewood-smoked bacon or other good bacon, chopped into ½-inch pieces
2	tablespoons minced shallots
¼	cup plus 2 tablespoons sherry vinegar
1¼	cups chicken broth
2	cups (¾-inch) cubes stale corn bread
2	cups roughly chopped chard
3	tablespoons butter
2	cups succotash (any combination of whatever is in season – corn, peas, lima beans, sugar snap peas, fava beans and/or chopped green beans)
4	tablespoons unsalted butter
1-2	tablespoons chopped chives

Brush the trout with a little olive oil, sprinkle with salt and pepper, and season generously with cumin and chile powder.

In a large skillet, cook the bacon until crisp. Remove the bacon and set aside. Drain all but 1 tablespoon of the bacon grease. Add the shallots and cook until golden brown. Add the vinegar and broth, stirring constantly. Return the bacon to the skillet. Boil the mixture until reduced by half. Season with salt and pepper.

In another large skillet, melt the 3 tablespoons of butter and cook the cornbread and chard until the chard is softened. Add a little broth to the cornbread mixture to soften it a little, if needed. Add salt, pepper, cumin and red chile to taste.

Cook the succotash in a saucepan with a little water and butter until crisp-tender. Season with salt and pepper.

Add the 4 tablespoons of unsalted butter and chives to the simmering bacon vinaigrette. Whisk until the butter is melted and combined.

Grill or pan-fry the trout until done to your taste. Place piles of the cornbread mixture on each plate. Halve the trout on the diagonal and rest it against the cornbread. Spoon bacon vinaigrette over and around the trout on each plate. Spoon the succotash onto the plate next to the trout. Serve immediately.

Courtesy of Q's Restaurant

Tagliatelle with Crispy Salmon, Sautéed Asparagus and Fresh Tomato Sauce

This dish is an experience for any palate. The flavors are distinct yet blend beautifully.

Serves
4 to 6

3 pounds Roma tomatoes, tops cut off and quartered
3 tablespoons red wine vinegar
3 cloves garlic; 2 cloves crushed, 1 clove very thinly sliced
Kosher salt
8-12 ounces salmon fillet, cut into 2x1-inch pieces
3 tablespoons chopped tarragon
1 tablespoon chopped Italian parsley
Freshly ground black pepper
5 tablespoons olive oil
1 pound tagliatelle or fettuccine
1 pound asparagus, chopped into 2-inch pieces
½ cup heavy cream
2 tablespoons grated Parmesan cheese
Italian parsley sprigs, for garnish

Put the tomatoes, vinegar and crushed garlic in a non-reactive bowl. Add salt to taste. Marinate for at least 2 hours and up to 24 hours. Purée the tomatoes, then adjust the seasonings and refrigerate, covered, until ready to serve (this may be done up to 2 days ahead).

In a small bowl, mix the tarragon, parsley and black pepper. Add 2 tablespoons of olive oil and stir to form a paste. Add the salmon and stir to coat well.

Bring a pot of water to a boil. Heat a large non-stick skillet over high heat. When the pan is very hot, add the salmon and sear on all sides (do not cook the salmon all the way through or it will be dry). Remove the salmon from the pan and keep warm. Cook the pasta until just *al dente*, about 8 to 9 minutes.

While the pasta is cooking, heat the remaining 3 tablespoons of olive oil in the skillet. Add the sliced garlic and brown slightly. Add the asparagus to the garlic, toss to combine and cook for 2 to 3 minutes. Drain the pasta and add it to the pan with the asparagus; toss to combine.

Whip the cream to soft peaks and fold in the Parmesan cheese. Put about ¼ cup of the tomato sauce into each pasta bowl. Twirl the pasta on a fork and place it in the center of the sauce. Arrange the asparagus and salmon around the pasta. Dollop the cream on the top of the pasta and garnish with parsley sprigs.

Courtesy of Chef Ben Davis, Tony's Meats & Specialty Foods

Rainbow Trout with Red Chile and Pecans

Cuisine Catering is a small, gourmet catering company located in Edwards, near Vail. They are actively involved in the Vail Valley community, participating in and supporting the Cinco de Mayo chili cook off, Edwards Harvest and a variety of other events. This is a fast and flavorful fish recipe. You can substitute almonds or macadamia nuts for the pecans. Or add pineapple or fruit salsa for a tropical trout.

Serves 4

4	rainbow trout
½	cup honey
1	tablespoon ground red chile
¼	cup chopped pecans
1	tablespoon vegetable oil
Lemon slices	

Clean the trout if necessary; rinse and pat dry. Lightly warm the honey and then stir in the chile. Brush the honey and chili mixture on the trout. Roll the trout in the pecans to coat.

Heat the oil in a skillet. Put the trout pecan side down in the pan and cook 3 for 5 minutes, until browned. Turn the trout and cook for 2 minutes more. Remove and serve immediately, garnished with lemon.

Courtesy of Cuisine Catering

Speidini con Pesce e Salsa Verde (Grilled Fish Skewers with Fresh Green Herb Sauce)

Chef Ben Davis' Farmers' Market class is a Saturday workshop at the Cherry Creek Fresh Market. Davis says, "The class walks the market, sampling, tasting and just exploring the produce. We purchase products based on what looks best and holds the most interest for the students. We then go to the Seasoned Chef Cooking School where I begin to formulate ideas and group the produce together. We cook entirely without recipes and the students really love the class – so much so that we have had to add a second class each year." This recipe pairs grilled fish with an Italian salsa verde constructed of fresh market herbs. The sauce also works beautifully with grilled chicken or vegetables.

Serves 4

8   (6 to 8 inch) rosemary skewers (or kabob skewers)
1   pound firm-fleshed white fish (sea bass, monkfish, halibut or scallops)
16 crimini mushrooms, cleaned, left whole
Olive oil
Kosher salt and black pepper
Salsa verde (recipe follows)

Strip the rosemary skewers of all but the very top of the green sprigs. Set aside. Cut the fish into 2-inch cubes. Clean the scallops, if using. Alternate the fish and mushrooms on the skewers, leaving about ¼ inch between each piece. Brush each skewer with olive oil. Grill for about 4 minutes on each side, seasoning each side with salt and pepper while on the grill. Serve with lemon wedges and salsa verde.

For the salsa verde:
1   bunch flat leaf parsley, leaves only
1   bunch basil, leaves only
½   bunch mint, leaves only
3   cloves garlic
½   cup capers
6   anchovy fillets
2   tablespoons red wine vinegar
5   tablespoons extra virgin olive oil
1   tablespoon Dijon mustard
Kosher salt and black pepper

In a food processor, pulse-chop the parsley, basil, mint, capers, garlic and anchovies and red wine vinegar until coarsely blended. Transfer to a bowl and drizzle in the olive oil, stirring constantly. Add the mustard and then season with salt and pepper. Allow to sit for 20 minutes before serving.

Courtesy of Chef Ben Davis, Tony's Meats & Specialty Foods

BREADS, SCONES, MUFFINS & BARS

Megan Miller's Scrumptious Pumpkin Bread

Rock Creek Farm, home to the "U-Pick-Em Pumpkin Patch," is the largest pumpkin patch in Colorado. Every October, thousands of people from all over Colorado and the neighboring states come to Rock Creek Farm in search of the perfect pumpkin. With 150 acres of brilliant, orange pumpkins to choose from, they can be sure to find their perfect pumpkin. In addition to pumpkins, customers return year after year for delicious pumpkin baked goods. This pumpkin bread is such a popular item it is hard to keep up with the demand for it. People are always asking for the secret family recipe, but it has never been revealed – until now! This bread tastes even better a day later. It also freezes well.

Makes
1 loaf

1¼	cups cooked, puréed pumpkin (or use canned pumpkin)
⅓	cup water
2	eggs
½	cup vegetable oil
1½	cups sugar
½	teaspoon nutmeg
2	teaspoons cinnamon
¾	teaspoon salt
1	teaspoon baking soda
1¾	cups flour
½	cup chopped walnuts (optional)

Preheat the oven to 350°F. In a large mixing bowl, combine the pumpkin, water, eggs, oil and sugar. Mix until well combined. Add the remaining ingredients and beat the mixture until smooth. Pour into a greased loaf pan. Bake for 60 to 65 minutes, or until a toothpick inserted in the middle of the loaf comes out clean.

Courtesy of Rock Creek Farm

Cranapple Scones

Bluepoint Bakery was founded in 1987 by two chefs, Fred Bramhall and Mary Clark, who have over 40 years of combined experience in some of Denver's finest restaurants. They established the bakery to produce fine breads as well as hand-made desserts. Using only the highest quality ingredients, Bluepoint makes fresh baked breads, rolls, muffins, danish, scones, croissants, pies, tarts, cakes and tortes. Almost any combination of dried fruit, fresh fruit and/or nuts, such as apricot-almond, strawberry or peach-blackberry, can be substituted for the apples and cranberries in this scone recipe.

Makes
8 scones

2¼	cups flour
¼	cup plus 2 tablespoons sugar
2	teaspoons baking powder
⅜	teaspoon baking soda
¼	teaspoon salt
1	stick plus 1 tablespoon unsalted butter
3	ounces cream cheese
1	egg, lightly beaten
½	cup buttermilk
2	ounces frozen and sliced cranberries
2	ounces apple, sliced and peeled

Preheat the oven to 425°F. Combine the flour, sugar, baking powder, baking soda and salt in a bowl. Add the butter and cream cheese. Mix with a paddle (or cut in by hand as in a pie dough) until crumbly. Add the buttermilk and half of the egg; mix just to combine. Add the cranberries and apples; mix just to distribute.

Roll out the dough about 1-inch thick and cut into triangles or rounds. Place on a papered or greased sheet pan and brush with the remaining beaten egg. Bake for 20 to 25 minutes, until lightly browned.

Courtesy of Bluepoint Bakery

Bavarian Snitzbrod

Mountain Mama flour is made from fine high altitude spring wheat organically grown at 7,600 feet in the Colorado Rockies. The wheat is freshly ground at low temperatures with stone-burr mills to preserve the natural enzymes and vitamins. Nothing is removed from the flour; likewise no preservatives or conditioners are added. What you get is freshly ground, 100 percent whole wheat flour, made by the people who grew the wheat. There is no better commercial flour available. This hearty bread is filled with flavor as well as nutrition. It tastes especially good lightly toasted with a little butter melted on top.

1	cup dried apricots
1	cup prunes
4	tablespoons yeast
½	cup warm water
½	cup melted butter or vegetable oil
1¼	cup honey
1	teaspoon salt
8	cups Mountain Mama whole wheat flour
1¼	cups golden raisins
1	cup chopped walnuts
2	teaspoons grated lemon zest
1	teaspoon ground cloves
¼	teaspoon ground ginger
¼	teaspoon nutmeg
3	eggs, lightly beaten

Cover the apricots and prunes with water and soak overnight. Remove the apricots and prunes, chop and set aside, reserving the soaking liquid. Add enough water to the soaking liquid to make 3 cups of liquid.

Put the yeast in a large bowl and pour in the water. Let the yeast soften for 5 minutes then stir to dissolve. Add the 3 cups soaking mixture, butter, honey, and salt and mix well. Mix in 5 cups of flour, a cup at a time. Mix in thoroughly after each cup. Cover bowl with a cloth and let the mixture rise until it is very bubbly.

Add the eggs and mix well. Add the raisins, walnuts, lemon zest, cloves, ginger, nutmeg and the apricots and prunes. Mix well to distribute all of the ingredients evenly, Add enough flour to produce a dough that is just slightly sticky. Knead for 10 minutes, then cover and let sit until the dough has doubled in size

Grease 6 to 8 small (3½x7½-inch) loaf pans. Preheat the oven to 325°F. Punch down the dough and divide it into 6 to 8 equal parts. Roll each part into a cylinder shape and place in a loaf pan. Cover all of the pans and let the dough rise again. When the dough forms mounds over the rim of the pans, put in the oven. Bake for about 1 hour, until the loaves sound hollow when tapped on the bottom. You may need to cover the tops with foil if they get too brown during baking.

Courtesy of Mountain Mama Flour

Very Lemon Bread

A lemony bread perfect for coffee, a morning meeting or afternoon tea. Note: if you cannot find lemon oil, you can make it by combining 2 teaspoons of canola oil with a couple of strips of lemon zest. Heat it over low heat for 3 minutes, then seal in a glass or plastic container and refrigerate overnight. Or you can also use 1½ teaspoons of lemon extract.

Makes
1 loaf

1	stick butter, at room temperature
1½	teaspoons lemon oil
2	cups sugar
3	eggs, at room temperature, lightly beaten
2¼	cups flour
1½	teaspoons baking powder
¾	teaspoon salt
¾	cup milk
3	tablespoons grated lemon zest
¾	cup chopped pecans
¼	cup fresh lemon juice
½	cup sugar

Preheat the oven to 350°F. In a large bowl, mix the butter, lemon oil, eggs and 1½ cups of sugar. In a separate bowl, sift the flour, baking powder and salt together. Add the flour mixture and the milk alternately to the butter mixture, one-third at a time, stirring just enough to blend. Fold in the lemon zest and pecans.

Pour the batter into a greased loaf pan and bake for 1 hour, or until a toothpick inserted in the center of the loaf comes out clean. Remove the bread from the pan. Poke holes at 1-inch intervals on all sides with a toothpick.

Combine the lemon juice and ½ cup of sugar to make a glaze. While the loaf is still warm, drizzle the lemon glaze over top and sides. Wrap the loaf in foil and store for 1 day before slicing to serve.

Courtesy of Maggie McCullough's Bakery and Cafe

Pumpkin Muffins with Streusel Topping

Mary Tigges has seen a lot of change in 80 years, but there is one thing that still doesn't change, and that is the "outrageous, delicious taste of fresh produce and the joy of eating off the land." Tigges Farm consists of 3,000 pepper plants in dozens of varieties, 1,000 tomato plants, a 20-acre pumpkin patch, sweet corn, Indian corn, broom corn, cucumbers, gourds and summer and winter squash. These delicious muffins have a cream cheese surprise in the middle. Note: serve the muffins immediately and refrigerate any leftovers. Food safety requires that products with cream cheese to be refrigerated if the product is going to be at room temperature for more than 1 hour.

Makes
24 muffins

3½ cups flour
1 cup packed light brown sugar
1 tablespoon baking powder
1½ teaspoons cinnamon
1 teaspoon salt
1 teaspoon nutmeg
2 eggs, beaten
1¼ cups cooked, puréed pumpkin (or use canned pumpkin)
1 cup milk
⅔ cup vegetable oil
8 ounces cream cheese, divided into 24 pieces
Streusel topping (recipe follows)

Preheat the oven to 375°F. Sift the flour, brown sugar, baking powder, cinnamon, salt and nutmeg into a bowl. In a separate bowl, mix the eggs and pumpkin. Add the milk and oil; mix again. Add the flour mixture and stir until just moistened. Fill paper-lined muffin cups half-full. Place 1 piece of cream cheese on the batter in each muffin cup and top with the remaining batter. Sprinkle with the streusel topping. Bake for 20 to 25 minutes, or until lightly browned.

For the streusel topping:
½ cup packed brown sugar
1 teaspoon cinnamon
2 tablespoons butter, melted
½ cup finely chopped walnuts

Mix all of the ingredients together.

Courtesy of Arapahoe County Cooperative Extension Food Preservation Specialist, Sergia Dunlap, Littleton, Colorado / Tigges Farm

Zucchini Bread

"The most frequently asked question at our vegetable stand is, how much of this zucchini will I need for most recipes. The answer is: one medium zucchini (⅓ pound) yields approximately two cups sliced or 1½ cups shredded zucchini." – Kathy Rickart, Tigges Farm.

3	eggs, beaten
2	cups sugar
2	teaspoons vanilla
1	teaspoon almond extract
1	cup vegetable oil
2	cups grated zucchini
3	cups flour
½	teaspoon baking powder
1	teaspoon salt
1	teaspoon baking soda
1	teaspoon cinnamon
½	cup chopped walnuts, chopped
1	cup shredded or grated coconut (optional)

Preheat the oven to 350°F. Beat the eggs until light and fluffy. Add the sugar, vanilla, almond extract and oil. Blend well. Stir in the zucchini.

Sift together the flour, baking powder, salt, soda and cinnamon. Blend with the egg mixture. Fold in the nuts and coconut. Divide the batter between 2 greased and floured loaf pans. Bake for 1 hour.

Courtesy of Kathy Rickart, Windsor, Colorado / Tigges Farms

Zucchini Bars

These bars have a delicious cinnamon frosting and are great for a mid-morning snack or an afternoon treat.

Makes
12 big bars

1½ sticks butter
½   cup packed brown sugar
½   cup sugar
2   eggs
1   teaspoon vanilla
1   teaspoon salt
1¾ cups flour
1½ teaspoons baking powder
2   cups grated zucchini
1   cup shredded coconut
1   cup chopped walnuts
Cinnamon frosting (recipe follows)

Preheat the oven to 350°F. Cream the butter and sugars together. Beat in the eggs and vanilla. Stir in the salt, flour and baking soda. Add the zucchini, coconut and walnuts. Spread the batter into a greased 10x15-inch baking pan. Bake for 40 minutes. Frost with cinnamon frosting.

For the cinnamon frosting:
1   cup powdered sugar
2½   tablespoons milk
1½   tablespoons margarine
1   teaspoon vanilla
½   teaspoon cinnamon

Mix all of the ingredients together until smooth.

Recipe from Larimer County Cooperative Extension Master Food Preservers, Fort Collins, Colorado / Tigges Farms

PIES

Cherry Pie

Heinie's Market has been selling Colorado produce since 1950. The market is open from May through November, but July is the season for Colorado cherries.

Makes
1 pie

1½	cups sugar
3	tablespoons cornstarch
¼	teaspoon salt
4	cups pitted sour cherries
¼	teaspoon almond extract
1	tablespoon butter

Pie dough, enough for bottom and top crusts

In a large bowl, mix together the sugar, cornstarch and salt. Add the cherries and almond extract; mix well. Let sit for 15 minutes.

Preheat the oven to 400°F. Stir the cherry mixture and pour it into a deep dish pie crust. Dot with the butter. Roll out the top crust and place over the cherries. Trim and flute the edges of the crust and cut decorative slits in it. Bake until the crust is brown, about 40 to 50 minutes. Let cool for 15 minutes before slicing.

Courtesy of Heinie's Market.

Rhubarb Pie

"We bought an acre of bean farm in 1951. We built a house in our spare time over the next eight years – materials: $10,000; land: $1,500; labor: $2.00; mortgage: $0.00. We grow squash, gladiolas, grapes, peaches and ornamental corn. Small operation … big satisfaction. This is my favorite rhubarb pie. It's very easy and is delicious with a little strawberry or vanilla ice cream." — Mercedes Morrison

Makes
1 Pie

3	tablespoons flour
1	cup sugar
1	egg, beaten
2	cups fresh or frozen rhubarb, cut into 1-inch pieces
1	9-inch unbaked pie crust with top crust

Preheat the oven to 425°F. Sift the flour and sugar together. Add the egg and mix thoroughly. Stir in the rhubarb. Fill the pie crust with the rhubarb mixture. Cover with a top crust or lattice and bake for 10 minutes. Reduce the heat to 350°F and bake for 35 more minutes, or until the crust is golden brown.

Courtesy of Morrison's Back Acker

Mary Tigges' Cinderella Pumpkin Pie

One of the best pumpkins to use for pies and other baked goods is the Rouge Uif D'Etampes, an antique French heirloom variety, better known as the "Cinderella" pumpkin. It earned its nickname from its shape, which looks very much like the pumpkin coach Cinderella rode to the ball.

Makes
1 pie fit
for Prince
Charming

3	eggs, beaten
½	cup packed brown sugar
½	cup sugar
1	teaspoon cinnamon
½	teaspoon nutmeg
¼	teaspoon ground cloves
¼	teaspoon salt
1	tablespoon butter, melted
1½	cups cooked, puréed fresh pumpkin (or canned pumpkin)
1½	cups light cream or evaporated milk
1	9-inch pie crust

Preheat the oven to 425°F. Combine the eggs and sugars with the cinnamon, nutmeg, cloves and salt. Add the melted butter, pumpkin and cream; mix well. Pour into the pie crust and bake for 15 minutes.

Lower the oven temperature to 350°F and bake for 40 more minutes, or until a knife inserted 1-inch from the pie's edge comes out clean. Cool before slicing.

Courtesy of Tigges Farms

Special Peach Pie

Some of the first peach trees in the Palisade area were planted in 1882. By the early 1900s, more than 25,000 pounds of peaches were being shipped daily from Palisade to destinations around the region. Today, Palisade peaches have a national reputation, and they are celebrated each August at the Palisade Peach Festival on Colorado's Western Slope. This pie won the Grand Prize at the 2000 Palisade Peach Festival for Michelle Plumb, who shares it with us. The touch of cinnamon in the crust spices up the fresh peach and sour cream filling.

For the crust:

Makes
1 pie

1¾	cups flour
¼	cup sugar
1	teaspoon cinnamon
½	teaspoon salt
1	stick plus 1 tablespoon butter, chilled
¼	cup ice water

Combine the flour, sugar, cinnamon and salt in a medium bowl. Cut in the butter until the mixture resembles a coarse meal. Add the water and stir gently with a fork until the dough is evenly moistened. Put the dough in the refrigerator for 10 minutes. Then remove the dough from the refrigerator and roll it into a circle slightly larger than a deep 10-inch deep-dish pie plate. Ease the pastry into a pie plate; trim any excess dough and form decorative edges with your fingers.

For the filling:

1	egg, lightly beaten
2	tablespoons vanilla
1⅔	cups sour cream
1	cup sugar
⅓	cup flour
Pinch of salt	
8	medium peaches, peeled, pitted and sliced
Streusel topping	

Preheat the oven to 450°F. In a large bowl, combine the egg, vanilla and sour cream. Add the sugar, flour and salt; mix to combine. Fold in the peaches. Put the peach mixture into the pie crust and bake for 10 minutes. Lower the oven temperature to 350°F and bake for about 40 minutes, until the filling is slightly puffed and golden brown. When the pie is done, remove it from the oven. Sprinkle the topping over the pie and bake it for 15 more minutes. Cool for 15 minutes before slicing.

For the topping:

1   cup chopped walnuts
⅓   cup flour
⅓   cup sugar
⅓   cup packed brown sugar
1   tablespoon cinnamon
Pinch of salt
1   stick butter, chilled

Combine the walnuts, flour, sugars, cinnamon and salt in a bowl; mix well. Blend in the butter until the mixture is crumbly.

Courtesy of Palisade Peach Festival

Cheddar Pear Pie

First Fruits Organic Farms grows organic apples, cherries, peaches, nectarines, pears and raspberries. They also make jams, dried fruit and fruit leather, fresh and frozen apple juice and applesauce. This is a different take on the traditional apple and cheddar cheese pie. Use a milder cheddar, as a sharp cheddar tends to overwhelm, rather than complement, the subtler flavor of the pear.

Makes
1 pie

4   large, ripe pears, peeled, cored and thinly sliced
1   tablespoon cornstarch
⅓   cup plus ¼ cup sugar
⅛   teaspoon plus ¼ teaspoon salt
1   unbaked 9-inch pie crust
½   cup grated cheddar cheese (not sharp cheddar)
½   cup flour
½   stick butter
¼   teaspoon salt

Preheat the oven to 425°F. In a bowl, combine the pears, cornstarch, ⅓ cup of sugar and ⅛ teaspoon of salt. Pour into the pie crust.

In a separate bowl, combine the cheese, flour, butter, ¼ teaspoon of salt and ¼ cup of sugar. Mix until crumbly; sprinkle over the pear filling.

Bake for 25 to 35 minutes, until the crust is golden brown and the cheese has melted. Cool on wire rack for 10 minutes. Serve warm.

Courtesy of First Fruits Organic Farms

Apple Apple Pie

This pie won the silver medal at the 1997 National Pie Championships in the Amateur Division, Traditional Apple Pie. The author admits that this is not health food. She uses an old-fashioned lard and vinegar pastry recipe for the tender, flaky crust (don't worry, there is no vinegar taste in the finished product). Two kinds and textures of apples are used to make this unique, prize winning pie.

For the pastry:

2	cups flour
½	teaspoon salt
1	stick unsalted butter, chilled and cut into 8 pieces
3	tablespoons cold lard, cut into small pieces
1	tablespoon distilled white vinegar
4-5	tablespoons ice water

Place the flour and salt in a food processor. Add the butter and lard; pulse a few times until the fat is in ¼-inch pieces (this can be done by hand).

Mix the vinegar and 2 tablespoons of water; add it to the flour mixture. Pulse 2 or 3 times to distribute the liquid. Add another 2 tablespoons of water and pulse several times until the water is well distributed. The mixture should hold together when pressed with your fingers. Add more water, a teaspoon at a time, if the dough is too dry.

Put the mixture onto a work surface and gather it together into a ball. Using the heel of your hand, quickly smear the dough across the work surface several times. This will blend the butter and lard. Do not over work the dough or it will become tough. Form the dough into a round, flat disk and wrap in plastic. Refrigerate the dough for at least 1 hour.

Let the dough sit out for a few minutes to warm it up before working with it. Roll out half the dough for the bottom crust and place it in a 9-inch deep dish pie pan.

For filling one:

3	Granny Smith apples (about 1 pound), peeled, cored and chopped
1	tablespoon fresh lemon juice
1	stick plus 2 tablespoons unsalted butter
Large pinch of salt	
⅓	cup golden brown sugar
¼	teaspoon freshly grated nutmeg
2	tablespoons dark rum
½	teaspoon vanilla

Combine the apples, lemon juice, unsalted butter, salt, brown sugar and nutmeg in a medium saucepan. Cover and cook over medium-low heat for 30 to 40 minutes, stirring occasionally. When the fruit is very soft and golden brown in color, stir in the rum and vanilla. Cook for 5 more minutes. Remove from the heat and mash the apples as you would for mashed potatoes. Season to taste with lemon juice, sugar, nutmeg or rum. Set aside.

For filling two:

5	Yellow Delicious apples, peeled, cored and thinly sliced
2	tablespoons fresh lemon juice
½	cup golden brown sugar
2	tablespoons flour (and more if needed)
1½	teaspoons cinnamon
Zest of 1 lemon, minced	
1½	teaspoons vanilla
¼	teaspoon freshly grated nutmeg
4	tablespoons butter, cut into small pieces

Toss the apples with the lemon juice and sugar. Allow the mixture to sit for a few minutes until the apples release their liquid. Add the flour and combine well (add more flour if the mixture is too soupy). Add the cinnamon, lemon zest, vanilla and nutmeg; blend well.

Preheat the oven to 350°F. Spread half the apple slices (filling 2) in the bottom crust. Top with all of the mashed apples (filling 1). Evenly place the remaining apple slices atop the mashed apples. Dot the apples with the butter.

Roll out the top crust. Cut vents in the dough (or small hearts or other shapes, reserving the shapes to place on the pie before baking). Place the top crust over the apples and trim the edges. Press the edges together to seal and form your favorite decorative edges. If using cut out shapes, place them decoratively atop the pie or inside the cut out shapes in the dough. Sprinkle the top with granulated sugar. Bake for 45 to 60 minutes, until the crust is golden brown and the apples are tender. Allow the pie to cool for 15 minutes before serving. The pie is great served warm with slices of cheddar cheese or vanilla ice cream.

Courtesy of Janis Judd, Contributing Author, Colorado Farmers' Market Cookbook

Apricots

In order to be full flavored, apricots must ripen on the tree, so it is always a relief when they make it though Colorado's frost-prone spring.

There are two varieties of apricots available at Colorado farmers' market. The Perfection is a large, oval fruit that is generally orange in color all over. The Riland is the pollinator and produces smaller fruit, which are round and very sweet, with a distinct reddish blush. Perfections ripen from the outside in, so they should look ripe when you buy them. Rilands ripen from the inside out, so even if the skin looks slightly green, they're ripe on the inside. Select apricots that have a little give. Keep them at room temperature until they are fully ripe, then store them in a plastic bag in the refrigerator for no more than two or three days.

If you think you don't like apricots, it may be because you've never tried one that was truly tree-ripened. Growers don't pick the fruit until it's ripe according to their taste test. If it makes them pucker, it stays on the tree. When it's sweet and juicy, it's picked and taken to the farmers' market.

Apricots, like many fruits, are best eaten fresh and unadorned. Always wash apricots before eating them. For variety, try slicing peeled and pitted apricots and placing them on a baking sheet. Cover the baking sheet with plastic wrap and put it in the freezer. After the apricots are frozen, store them air-tight in the freezer. To serve, add the frozen fruit to vanilla yogurt in the blender and blend until smooth. Spoon the mixture into wine glasses or small bowls for a cooling treat.

Another idea is to dice apricots and add small handfuls to the top side of pancakes when they reach the bubbly stage. Gently press the apricots down with your spatula, then turn them over and cook the fruit side until set.

If you have a dehydrator, be sure to dry at least one batch of apricots. These are great eaten as a snack, or snipped into small pieces and added to granola or oatmeal for an energy-packed breakfast.

Apricot Cake / Serves 6

This cake is one of those "never fail" desserts that can be made quickly, pleases everyone and, best of all, looks like you slaved! The cake is best eaten warm.

1	cup flour
1	teaspoon baking powder
¼	teaspoon salt
2	tablespoons plus ½ cup sugar
2½	tablespoons butter, chilled; plus 1½ tablespoons butter, melted
1	egg
½	teaspoon vanilla
Milk	
4	cups washed, sliced apricots
½	teaspoon cinnamon

Preheat the oven to 425°F. Grease an 8-inch or 9-inch round cake pan. Sift together the flour, baking powder, salt and 2 tablespoons of sugar. Cut the 2 tablespoons of chilled butter into the mixture until it looks crumbly.

In a measuring cup, beat the egg and vanilla, then add enough milk to make ½ cup. Combine with the flour mixture to make a stiff dough. Press down into the cake pan with floured hands. Arrange the apricot slices in overlapping circles around the pan until the dough is covered.

Combine ½ cup sugar, cinnamon and melted butter, and sprinkle over the apricots (use less of the sugar mixture for a less sweet cake). Bake for 20 minutes, until a toothpick inserted in the center of the cake comes out clean. Slice in wedges and remove with pie server.

Article and recipe courtesy of Laura Korth, Longmont Farmers' Market

I Can't Believe it's Sugarless Apple Pie

Ela Family Farms is located on a tranquil mesa near Hotchkiss, a small town nestled in the mountains of western Colorado. The Ela family has been growing fruit in the area since 1920. As fourth generation growers, the Ela's continue to plant new varieties, try new ideas and nurture their trees to produce fruits with an unmatched explosion of flavor and brilliance of color. This pie is a healthy dessert that uses the natural sugar found in apple juice concentrate as the sweetener. We were a bit skeptical when testing this recipe, but you definitely do not miss the added sugar, and if anything, the flavors of apple and cinnamon are even more pronounced than in typical apple pies – highly recommended.

Makes
1 pie

1	6-ounce can unsweetened apple juice concentrate
6	medium apples, peeled, cored and thinly sliced
3	tablespoons cornstarch
2	tablespoons cold water
1	tablespoon butter
1	teaspoon cinnamon
1	unbaked deep-dish pie crust with top crust

Preheat the oven to 425°F. Bring the apple juice concentrate to a boil in a saucepan. Add the apples and cook until crisp-tender.

Dissolve the cornstarch in the cold water. Add the cornstarch mixture, butter and cinnamon to the apples; stir well. Pour the apple mixture into the pie crust. Cover with the top crust. Press the edges of the crust together and form a decorative edge around the pie. Bake for 10 minutes. Reduce the oven temperature to 350°F and bake for 30 more minutes. When the crust is lightly browned and the apples are tender, remove the pie from the oven and let cool before serving.

Courtesy of Ela Family Farms

Peach-Raspberry Pie with Pecan Crust

Peaches and raspberries are a match made in heaven. Sunshine Hetzel won First Prize at the 1999 Palisade Peach Festival with this creation. Don't be put off by the vinegar in the crust, it makes the crust tender and you cannot taste it in the finished pie.

For the crust:

Makes
1 pie

1	cup finely chopped pecans
2¾	cups flour
1	teaspoon salt
⅓	teaspoon nutmeg
3	sticks butter, chilled and cut into pieces
1	teaspoon vinegar
1	egg, beaten
⅓	cup milk

Combine the pecans, flour, salt and nutmeg in a mixing bowl. Cut in the butter until the mixture has the consistency of coarse meal. Mix the vinegar, egg and milk together, then add to the flour mixture. Mix with a fork to moisten and form into a ball with your hands. Cover with plastic wrap and chill for 30 to 60 minutes.

For the filling:

6	generous cups peeled and sliced peaches
2	cups fresh raspberries (or 10-ounce package frozen raspberries, thawed and drained)
1	teaspoon vanilla
1	teaspoon cinnamon
1	teaspoon nutmeg
½	cup flour
⅔	cup sugar

Preheat the oven to 350°F. In a large bowl, lightly toss the peaches and raspberries with the vanilla. Mix in the cinnamon, nutmeg, flour and sugar. Set aside.

Roll out half the dough. Place it in a deep-dish pie pan. Put the filling in the crust. Roll out the other half of the dough and cover the filling with it. Crimp the crust's edges. Make a few small slits in the top crust. Cover the crust's edge with foil and bake for 40 to 50 minutes. Remove the foil from the crust's edge during the last 15 to 20 minutes of baking. When the crust is golden brown and the filling is bubbling, the pie is done. Let sit for 20 minutes before slicing.

Courtesy of Palisade Peach Festival

Creamy Pear Pie Crunch

Ela Family Farms grows organic fruit – eight varieties of apples, seven varieties of peaches and super-sweet pears. They sell their fruit, jams and cider in several Denver-area farmers' markets and select produce stands. The Ela's also offer gift boxes of peaches, pears and apples that can be shipped nationwide. This recipe is a cross between a pie and a crisp. It is a late-fall and early-winter family favorite.

Serves
10 to 12

¾ cup sugar
1 tablespoon cornstarch
¼ teaspoon cinnamon
⅛ teaspoon nutmeg (optional)
⅛ teaspoon salt
½ cup heavy cream
1 tablespoon lemon juice
2½ cups peeled, cored and chopped pears
1 cup packed brown sugar, or more to your taste
1 cup flour
1 cup rolled oats (not instant oats)
¼ teaspoon baking powder
1 stick butter, melted

Preheat the oven to 425°F. In a large bowl, mix the sugar, cornstarch, cinnamon, nutmeg and salt. Add the cream and lemon juice; mix well. Add the pears and gently stir to combine. Put the mixture into a greased 8x8-inch baking pan.

In a separate bowl, mix the brown sugar, flour, oatmeal and baking powder. Mix in the butter and sprinkle over the pear mixture. Bake for 30 to 35 minutes, until the brown sugar topping is browned and the pears are tender.

Courtesy of Ela Family Farms

DESSERTS

Colorado Cherry Crumbles

Carbondale's Restaurant six89 has been getting rave reviews nationally for its creative, regionally-influenced menu. The restaurant uses in-season ingredients from local farmers' markets and, in addition, contracts with several North Fork and Palisade farmers to have produce grown for them. These cherry crumbles are excellent served warm with ginger or vanilla ice cream and fresh whipped cream.

Serves 6

2½   pounds Colorado cherries, washed, stemmed and pitted
1   cup sugar
1   cup flour
1½   teaspoons kosher salt
½   teaspoon cinnamon
1   tablespoon fresh lemon juice
½   teaspoon cayenne
Crumble topping (recipe follows)

Toss the cherries with the sugar and let sit for 30 minutes.

Preheat the oven to 375°F. Add the flour, salt, cinnamon, lemon juice and cayenne to the cherries; toss gently to coat.

Divide the cherry mixture among 6 ramekins (or an 8x8-inch baking dish). Top with the crumble topping. Put the ramekins on baking sheets (or put the baking dish in the oven) and bake for 20 minutes, or until the top is lightly browned and the filling is bubbling.

For the crumble topping:
2   cups flour
1   cup sugar
1   cup packed light brown sugar
½   teaspoon kosher salt
2   sticks unsalted butter, cut into pieces
1   cup chopped, toasted walnuts

Mix the flour, sugars and salt. Cut in the butter until the mixture resembles a coarse meal. Add the walnuts; mix well. Refrigerate until ready to use.

Courtesy of Restaurant six89

Ruth's Chocolate Zucchini Cake

This wonderfully moist cake is a perfect way to use up that extra zucchini. This cake was good on the first day, but the next day ... it was better! To make sour milk, mix ½ cup milk with 1½ teaspoons lemon juice or vinegar and let sit for 5 minutes.

Serves 12 to 14

½	cup buttermilk or sour milk
1	teaspoon baking soda
1	stick butter or margarine, at room temperature
1	teaspoon salt
1¾	cups sugar
1	teaspoon vanilla
½	cup vegetable oil
2	eggs
2½	cups flour
1½	teaspoons baking powder
¼	cup unsweetened cocoa
2	cups grated zucchini
1	cup chopped walnuts
1	cup chocolate chips (optional)

Preheat the oven to 350°F. In a small bowl, combine the buttermilk and baking soda; stir until the baking soda has dissolved. In a separate bowl, mix the butter, salt, sugar, vanilla, oil and eggs. Add the buttermilk mixture and mix well.

Combine the flour, baking powder, cocoa, zucchini and walnuts; add them to the egg mixture and mix well. Pour the batter into a greased 9x13-inch baking pan. Bake for 40 to 50 minutes, until a toothpick inserted in the center of the cake comes out clean.

If desired, at the end of the baking, sprinkle the cake with the chocolate chips and return to oven until they are just melted to "frost" the cake.

Courtesy of Front Range Organic Gardeners

Grilled Apricots and Chèvre with Ice Wine Sauce

This sophisticated, but simple, European-inspired summer dessert uses only Colorado products. It is also excellent using fresh peaches instead of apricots. The dessert wine in the recipe comes from the award-winning Plum Creek Cellars in Palisade. Founded in 1984, Plum Creek was one of Colorado's first wineries. Today, the winery produces Chardonnay, Merlot, Sangiovese, Cabernet Franc, Cabernet Sauvignon and Riesling Ice Wine.

Serves 4

4   fresh Colorado apricots
2   cups Colorado Plum Creek Cellars Riesling Ice Wine, or other sweet
    dessert wine
8   ounces Haystack Mountain spreadable goat cheese (*fromage blanc*)
Fresh mint leaves

Preheat the grill. Halve the apricots and cut 3 to 4 shallow slices in the skin of the fruit. Put the apricots in a zip-lock bag and add wine to cover. Seal the bag and allow the fruit to soak in the wine for 1 to 3 hours. Remove the apricots; reserve the wine. Put the apricots on a preheated grill pan or clean gas grill grate and grill until the apricots are marked with grill marks and are heated through.

Put the reserved wine in a small saucepan over medium heat. Simmer the wine until it reduces and thickens to a glaze-like consistency. To serve, place the warm apricots on attractive dessert plates. Top with a dollop of goat cheese, drizzle with the warm wine glaze and garnish with mint leaves.

Courtesy of Chef Mick Rosacci, Tony's Meats & Specialty Foods

Upside-Down Raspberry Cake

This moist, delicious cake, full of fresh, sweet raspberries, is sure to be a hit at your house.

1½ cups fresh raspberries (or frozen, unthawed raspberries)
2   sticks butter, at room temperature
1   cup sugar
3   eggs
2   teaspoons fresh lemon juice
1   teaspoon vanilla
2   cups flour
1½ teaspoons baking powder
½   teaspoon salt
⅔   cup milk
Powdered sugar

Preheat the oven to 350°F. Line the bottom of the baking pan with parchment or waxed paper and coat lightly with cooking spray. Evenly distribute ½ cup of the raspberries in the bottom of the baking pan and set aside.

In a large mixing bowl, cream the butter and the sugar together. Add the eggs, lemon juice and vanilla. Mix well. In a separate bowl, combine the flour, baking powder and salt. Alternately stir the flour mixture and the milk into the butter mixture, using about one-third each time. Gently fold in the remaining 1 cup of raspberries. Carefully pour the batter over the raspberries in the baking pan.

Bake for 40 to 45 minutes, or until a toothpick inserted in the center comes out clean. Let cool a few minutes, then run a knife around the edges of the cake. Invert the cake onto a platter and carefully remove the parchment or wax paper. Cool completely. Dust with powered sugar and serve.

Courtesy of Straw Hat Farm

Boulder Chèvre Cheesecake

This recipe was inspired by Emily Luchetti, the talented executive pastry chef of Farallon Restaurant in San Francisco.

Serves
8 to 10

¾   pound Haystack Mountain goat cheese, at room temperature
¾   cup plus 2 tablespoons sugar
1½   teaspoons fresh lemon juice
1   teaspoon minced lemon zest
1   teaspoon vanilla
6   large eggs, separated
3   tablespoons flour
3   large peaches, peeled, pitted and cut into ¼-inch slices
¼   cup blueberries
Powdered sugar
Whipped cream or crème fraîche (optional)

Preheat the oven to 350°F. Butter a 9-inch round cake pan (a springform pan works best) and dust with 1 tablespoon of sugar.

In a mixing bowl, combine the cheese, ¾ cup of sugar, lemon juice, lemon zest and vanilla. Beat at medium speed until smooth. Beat in the egg yolks, one at a time, incorporating each one completely before adding the next. Turn the mixer to low and add the flour.

In another mixing bowl, using clean beaters, beat the egg whites until firm. Beat one-third of the egg whites into the cheese mixture. Gently fold in the rest of the egg whites. Spoon the batter into the cake pan; bake for 35 to 45 minutes, until a toothpick inserted in the center of the cheesecake comes out clean and the cake is a deep golden brown (do not underbake it). Cool for 15 minutes on a wire rack. Carefully remove the cake from the pan onto a serving plate and cool completely.

In a medium bowl, combine the peaches and blueberries with 1 tablespoon of sugar (more or less, depending on the sweetness of the fruit). Set aside.

When ready to serve, dust the cheesecake with powdered sugar and spoon the fruit on top of the cake, leaving a 1-inch border all the way around. Cut and serve, garnishing each piece with a little whipped cream.

Courtesy of Haystack Mountain Goat Dairy

Peaches

Few things are as eagerly anticipated as the first of the Colorado peaches, fresh from the tree. A fresh peach is simplicity itself and can be enjoyed with no effort greater than a quick rinse to remove the fuzz. Yet, the peach is one of the most versatile fruits around. It can be dried, canned, frozen, jammed, pickled (but why would you do that to a peach?), baked, broiled and pureed.

For six weeks beginning in August, at least eleven varieties of freestone peaches can be found at your farmers' market. Peach growers offer sampling so that you can decide right then and there which peach is best suited for your canning, jam, cobbler, etc. They are sold in quantities ranging from snack bags to boxes and most allow you to mix and match varieties if you'd like. Now that's customer service!

Make a breakfast parfait by layering fresh peaches with vanilla yogurt and granola in clear glasses or bowls. Or, fill a sherbet glass with sliced peaches and fresh raspberries and pour chilled, sparkling white grape juice over all for a delicious dessert!

As with many other fruits, peaches can easily be frozen by slicing them onto a baking sheet and freezing briefly, then transferring the frozen slices to freezer bags for storage. Frozen this way, the slices can be individually poured out and used for pies, cobblers, crisps, frozen yogurt, homemade ice cream, peach drinks and more.

The following recipe is quick and easy to accomplish – no ice cream maker needed! The sorbet is intended to be eaten with your meal to refresh and cleanse the palate. The texture should be somewhat icy. Try serving it with a spicy menu to fully appreciate its crisp, clean, light flavor. Or, serve it as a refreshing dessert.

Peach Sorbet / Serves 4

4-5 fresh peaches
1/2 cup sugar
1 tablespoon fresh lemon juice

Purée the peaches, sugar and lemon juice in food processor or blender. Freeze in a loaf pan until solid. Remove from the freezer and thaw slightly. Break into large chunks and place in a mixer bowl. Beat until well-blended but still frozen. Return the mixture to the loaf pan, cover and refreeze. Serve in small scoops, garnished with lemon balm or mint sprigs.

Bingham Hill Cheesecake

Bingham Hill's Plain Fresh and Simple cheese is similar to European Quark or American Baker's Cheese. According to Bingham Hill, "European chefs insist on using fresh cheeses, not cream cheese, for pastries – this is the way cheesecake is supposed to taste! Fresh and Simple cheese is made with gently pasteurized whole cow's milk and cream. It is a spreadable cheese which we developed with old-fashioned baker's cheese in mind. With only the bare minimum of ingredients, the fresh cheese flavor shines." Halved and pitted fresh sweet cherries, sliced strawberries, raspberries, blackberries or blueberries are delicious on top. If you do not have the time or inclination to make a shortcrust, use a pre-made one. The cheese filling will fill two 9-inch pre-made shortbread crusts and the cheesecake will be about 1¼-inches tall. You can halve the filling recipe if you want to make just one cheesecake with a store-bought crust.

Serves
10 to 12

For the shortcrust:
2   cups flour
½   cup powdered sugar
Pinch of salt
1   stick butter, chilled and cut into small pieces
1   egg yolk
1-2 tablespoons ice water

Sift the flour, powdered sugar and salt into a cold metal bowl. Cut in the butter. Mix the egg yolk with the water and stir into the flour with a fork, until the ingredients are mixed but crumbly. Knead the dough, working quickly so that the butter does not get too soft. Form the dough into a ball, wrap tightly in plastic wrap and place in the refrigerator for at least 1 hour.

Preheat the oven to 350°F. Roll the ball of chilled dough into a 13-inch diameter circle. Line a 10-inch, fluted tart pan with the dough. Crimp the sides and trim any extra dough. Pierce the base of the crust with a fork. Line the crust with foil, fill with dried lentils or baking weights to hold the crust in place and bake until light brown, about 10 minutes. Remove the crust from the oven and let cool.

For the cheese cake filling:
2½   cups Bingham Hill Plain Fresh and Simple cheese
4   eggs, separated
¾   cup sugar, divided
1   stick butter, melted
½   cup flour
Pinch of salt
1   teaspoon grated lemon zest

Preheat the oven to 300°F. Pour off any liquid (whey) from the cheese. Push the cheese through a strainer or food mill to fluff it. Whisk together the cheese, egg yolks and ¼ cup plus 2 tablespoons of sugar, beating until fluffy. Pour the melted butter into the cheese mixture in a thin stream, stirring constantly. Sift in the flour and add the salt and lemon zest; mix well.

Beat the egg whites with the remaining ¼ cup plus 2 tablespoons of sugar, until stiff peaks are formed. Carefully fold the egg whites into the cheese mixture. Pour the cheese filling into the baked pastry; smooth the filling evenly. Bake the cheesecake for 45 minutes, until golden brown. Cool completely (it's best if chilled overnight).

Courtesy of Bingham Hill Cheese Company

Sesame Honey Baked Fruit

César Flores produces all-natural honey that is unheated, unfiltered, unliquified, unpasteurized, unprocessed and unmolested. As Flores says, "It's straight from the hive!" This is a simple, rich, hot dessert featuring Flores Colorado honey. You can substitute a chopped banana for the apple (just drizzle the banana with the honey-tahini mixture and bake). Tahini is a Middle Eastern sesame paste available at most groceries.

Serves 2

2	large Colorado apples, such as Braeburns
½	cup sesame tahini
½	cup local honey, slightly warmed

Carefully cut off the top ½-inch of the apples and scoop out the core without puncturing the skin on the bottom. Thoroughly mix the tahini and honey. Divide the mixture between the apples and place in the hollowed-out apple. Put each apple in a small dessert bowl and bake, microwave or steam until the apples are tender. Garnish with a sprinkle of bee pollen or a drizzle of chocolate syrup.

Courtesy of César Flores, Beekeeper

Cherries

The saying may be "as American as apple pie," but it's more likely our forefathers were celebrating Independence Day in 1776 with a big 'ol slice of cherry pie. With cherries so lush and bountiful in early July, "as American as cherry pie" would seem equally fitting. Fresh cherries always seem to bring a smile to one's face.

The arrival of fresh cherries at the market announces that summer has officially arrived. Peaking in Colorado from mid-June to mid-July, cherries represent the first arrival of the prized local stone fruits. The others – plums, apricots and peaches – will all be arriving at the market during the next several weeks.

Buy cherries that are deep red, glossy, plump, firm and full-feeling, but not wet or sticky (sticky cherries are over-ripe and have begun giving off their juice). Look at the stems and skip cherries with brittle or dry stems.

Because cherries are picked ripe, their quality declines fairly quickly from picking day. Use cherries within two to three days of purchasing. Store them whole, with stems intact, in a dry plastic bag in the refrigerator. Before using, wash and remove the stems. Discard any cherries that are too soft. Like a lot of our local summer jewels, cherries will go from abundant to extinct in a matter of weeks. Enjoy them while you can!

Cherry Clafouti / Serves 4

This simple dessert from Provence uses an easy crepe-like batter. A cherry pitter will speed up the preparation.

2	tablespoons butter, melted and cooled to room temperature
3	eggs
1	tablespoon sugar
1	tablespoon honey
¼	teaspoon salt
¼	teaspoon cinnamon
3	tablespoons flour
1	teaspoon amaretto liqueur, or ¼ teaspoon almond extract
¼	teaspoon vanilla
¾	cup heavy cream
1	pound cherries, washed, stemmed and pitted
2-3	tablespoons powdered sugar

Preheat the oven to 350°F. Butter 4 small gratin dishes (or a 12-inch glass or ceramic baking dish). In a stainless steel mixing bowl, whisk together the eggs and sugar until slightly frothy. Stir in the honey, salt and cinnamon. Using a small sifter or strainer, sift the flour over the egg mixture. Whisk the flour into the eggs to form a smooth batter. Once the batter is lump-free, stir in the amaretto and vanilla, then the melted butter and heavy cream. Let the batter sit for 10 to 15 minutes.

Divide the cherries among the gratin dishes (or the baking dish), so that the cherries are close to one another, but not densely packed. Divide the batter among the dishes (about ½ cup of batter per dish), tilting and moving the dishes a bit to allow the batter to cover the cherries and settle to the bottom evenly. The cherries should be just poking through the top of the batter.

Place the gratin dishes on baking sheet and bake for 20 to 30 minutes, until the batter is just dry in center (the edges will puff and cook much more quickly). When the centers are set and springy, remove to a cooling rack for at least 15 minutes. Sift powdered sugar over the top and serve warm with ice cream.

Article and recipe courtesy of Sean Kelly, Claire de Lune

Raspberry Sandwich Cookies

Cotswold Cottage Foods is a small, Colorado-based gourmet food manufacturer. Founded in Denver in 1983 as an authentic British tea room, Cotswold Cottage specialized in scone mixes, jams, lemon curd mix, gingerbread mix and stuffing mixes. These cookies are a tea-time treat featuring Colorado jam.

Makes
10 cookies

½ stick butter
¼ cup sugar
1 cup flour
2 tablespoons ground almonds
1 egg
Cotswold Cottage raspberry jam
Powdered sugar

Preheat the oven to 400°F. Cream the butter and sugar together. Add the flour and ground almonds; mix well. Roll out the dough and cut it into 20 round shapes using a 2-inch cookie cutter. Bake for 12 minutes. Cool the cookies. Spread raspberry jam on one cookie and sandwich with another. Dust with powdered sugar.

Courtesy of Cotswold Cottage Foods

Wild Berry Crisp

This delicious crisp tastes best with a bounty of freshly picked raspberries and blackberries. You can use frozen or canned berries as well. Other combinations of fruit, such as peaches and apples, are also good – just use your imagination. Serve the crisp warm with vanilla ice cream. You can also use whipping cream and fresh berries as a garnish.

Serves
10 to 12

1 stick butter, at room temperature
1 cup packed brown sugar
¼ cup flour
3 cups granola
4 cups mixed berries, plus extra for garnish
1 teaspoon sugar
½ teaspoon powdered ginger
1 teaspoon cinnamon

Preheat the oven to 350°F. In a medium bowl, combine the butter, sugar, flour and granola. Coat an 8x8-inch baking pan with cooking spray. Put half of granola mixture in the pan. Cover the granola with the berries. Sprinkle the sugar, ginger and cinnamon over the berries, then top with the remaining granola mixture.

Cover the pan with aluminum foil and bake for 45 to 50 minutes. Remove the foil and bake for 10 more minutes, until lightly browned. Cool slightly and serve with vanilla ice cream and a garnish of fresh berries.

Courtesy of Cuisine Catering

Pumpkin Cookies

These cookies are a great alternative to ordinary chocolate chip cookies. They taste wonderful, are not too sweet and kids love them! They also freeze well.

Makes
12 to 16
cookies

2	cups flour
1	cup quick cooking oats (not instant oats)
½	teaspoon baking soda
1	heaping teaspoon cinnamon
¼	teaspoon pumpkin pie spice
½	teaspoon salt
1½	sticks butter, at room temperature
¾	cup packed brown sugar
½	cup sugar
1	egg
½	teaspoon vanilla
2	cups cooked, puréed pumpkin (or use canned pumpkin)
1	cup chocolate chips (optional)
1	cup chopped walnuts (optional)

Preheat the oven to 350°F. Combine the flour, oats, baking soda, cinnamon, pumpkin pie spice and salt. Set aside.

In another bowl, cream the butter and sugars together until fluffy. Add the egg and vanilla; beat well. Add the dry ingredients alternately with the pumpkin to the creamed mixture; mix well after each addition. Add the chocolate chips and walnuts. Mix just to combine.

Drop by tablespoon onto a greased cookie sheet. Bake for 10 to 15 minutes, or until lightly browned.

Courtesy of Rock Creek Farm

Orange Honey Cake

This is a very moist cake that tastes good by itself, or served with fresh fruit or a dollop of orange-flavored whipped cream. For an impressive dessert, make the cake in an angelfood cake pan and fill the center with fresh berries after it's done baking. Use this recipe in place of shortcake, or try toasting a slice of the cake – breakfast will never be the same. A hint for using honey is to warm it briefly in the microwave. This makes it easier to measure and to mix with other ingredients.

Makes 2
9-inch
cakes

2	cups cake flour
¾	teaspoon baking powder
½	teaspoon salt
1	stick butter
½	cup sugar
⅔	cup honey
3	egg yolks
½	cup orange juice
2	egg whites, beaten until stiff

Preheat the oven to 350°F. Spray two 9-inch round baking pans (or use a ring-mold or angelfood cake pan), with non-stick spray and then coat with flour.

Sift the flour once to measure, then add the baking powder and salt, and sift again. In a large mixing bowl, beat the butter and sugar until light and fluffy. Add the honey and mix well. Add the egg yolks one at a time and beat thoroughly after each. Add the flour mixture, alternating with the orange juice, one-third at a time, mixing well after each addition. Fold in the beaten egg whites.

Pour the batter into the prepared baking pans and bake for 30 to 35 minutes, until the cake begins to pull away from the sides of the pan. Cool slightly before unmolding. Serve warm or cool completely and serve at room temperature.

Courtesy of J&J Apiaries

Pumpkin Cake

Burritt's Produce is a Delta County farm that produces organic beets, cherries, apricots, bell peppers, carrots, chile peppers, cucumbers, green beans, potatoes, summer squash, sweet corn, tomatoes, zucchini and cantaloupe. They also raise pumpkins, which are used to make the following rich and moist cake. The cake is finished with a delicious cream cheese frosting. Don't expect to have any leftovers!

Makes
9x13-inch
cake

4	eggs
1	egg white
1⅓	cups sugar
¾	cup vegetable oil
1½	cups cooked, puréed pumpkin (or use canned pumpkin)
2¼	cups flour
1½	teaspoons baking powder
2	teaspoons cinnamon
1	teaspoon salt
1	teaspoon baking soda

Cream cheese frosting (recipe follows)

Preheat the oven to 350°F. Grease and flour a 9x13-inch baking pan. In a large mixing bowl, beat together the eggs, egg white, sugar, oil and pumpkin. Sift together the flour, baking powder, cinnamon, salt and baking soda; add to the pumpkin mixture and mix well. Pour the batter into the baking pan. Bake for 35 to 40 minutes, until a knife inserted in the center of the cake comes out clean. Allow the cake to cool before frosting.

For the cream cheese frosting:

8	ounces cream cheese, at room temperature
½	stick butter, at room temperature
2	cups powdered sugar
1	teaspoon vanilla
½	teaspoon almond extract

Beat all of the ingredients together until smooth.

Courtesy of Burritt's Produce

desserts **197**

Pears

Did you ever wonder why Bartlett pears are always picked green? Perhaps it's for ease of shipping. Or, maybe an over-anxious farmer just couldn't wait to pick his orchard. Would you have guessed that picking Bartlett pears green actually yields better-tasting fruit? Read on to learn how perfect sweetness and texture is achieved in a summer pear.

As harvest time nears in the pear orchards, growers begin testing their fruit for maturity. They use a pressure gauge with a special plunger to test a single pear on a single tree. When the plunger penetrates a pear at 16 pounds of pressure or less, the sugar content of that pear is considered to be at its peak and the tree is picked. Each tree in the orchard is tested and either picked or marked for later testing. If Bartlett pears were ripened of the tree until yellow, they would end up with a gritty texture, not the smooth flesh that we love so much.

Of course, Bartlett pears aren't meant to be eaten in the green, rock-hard stage. They need to spend time in a cool place, slowly turning a light yellow. To ripen pears at home, place them in a brown paper bag at room temperature for several days, checking them each day and removing any ripe ones to the refrigerator.

When pears are firm-ripe, they are ready for eating or canning. Prior to canning, call your local Extension office for free information on proper canning methods for your altitude. As the pears become riper (but not bruised or mushy), they are just right for dehydrating. Pears can be dehydrated in halves, quarters or slices. If you like your dried pears thoroughly dried, you can store them in your cupboard. If you prefer a softer texture, which indicates that there is still moisture in the fruit, store them airtight in the freezer. The softest of the pears can be used for making jam or fruit leather.

Here is a great breakfast idea, especially if you are in a hurry: spread a thin layer of cream cheese on a slice of whole wheat bread. Top with sliced pear and sprinkle with a mixture of cinnamon and sugar. Broil until done to your taste.

Honey Poached Pears / Serves 4

This basic preparation will produce pears that can be sliced to fill a tart or served whole with ice cream, cookies and a bit of honey syrup

4	Bartlett pears, peeled
2	cups water
2	cups white wine
½	cup honey
1	tablespoon finely chopped, peeled fresh ginger root
1	whole vanilla bean, split

Trim the bottom of the pears so they can stand upright. Leave the stem and core intact.

Bring the water and wine to a simmer. Stir in the honey, ginger and vanilla bean. Add the pears and simmer for 5 to 7 minutes, until tender but not mushy, moving them every so often to keep them submerged.

Test the pears periodically with a toothpick – the pears are done when the toothpick slides in with no resistance until it reaches the stem area. When the pears are done, use a slotted spoon to remove them gently to a plate. Place the pears in the refrigerator, uncovered, to cool.

Continue simmering the liquid, reducing and tasting until a light, sweet syrup is achieved. Pour the syrup through a strainer, discarding the ginger and vanilla. Cool the syrup for 30 minutes in the refrigerator. Add the pears to the syrup, cover and store in the refrigerator. Poached pears will keep for up to 3 days refrigerated in the syrup. Before serving, bring the pears to room temperature. Use in recipes or serve with the syrup.

Article courtesy of Laura Korth, Longmont Farmers' Market; Recipe courtesy of Sean Kelly, Claire de Lune

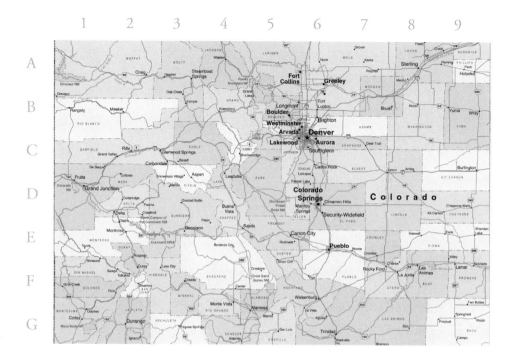

Colorado Farmers' Market Guide

Denver Metro

Aspen Park Farmers' Market   (B-5)
RTD Park & Ride and Highway 285 (before Conifer), Aspen Park
303-421-2076
Mid-June - Late September
Saturday, 10 a.m. - 2 p.m.

Aurora Farmers' Market   (B-5)
9800 E. Colfax Avenue, Aurora
303-361-6169
email: Daurorabus@aol.com
www.AuroraBusiness.org
Mid-June - First Frost
Saturday, 7 a.m. - sellout

Buckingham Square Mall Farmers' Market   (B-5)
S. Havana and Mississippi (by Beau Jo's Pizza), Aurora
Farmers' Market Hotline: 303-887-FARM
www.denverfarmersmarket.com
Late June - Late October
Tuesday, 11 a.m. - sellout

Boulder County Farmers' Market   (B-4)
13th Street between Canyon Boulevard and Arapahoe Avenue, Boulder
303-910-2236
www.boulderfarmers.org
Mid-May - Early October
Wednesday, 10 a.m. - 2 p.m.
Early April - Late October
Saturday, 8 a.m. - 2 p.m.

Castle Rock Farmers' Market   (C-5)
11 S. Wilcox Street (Across from the library), Castle Rock
Farmers' Market Hotline: 303-570-FARM
www.coloradofarmersmarket.com
Early June - September
Saturday, 8 a.m. - 2 p.m.

Centennial Farmers' Market   (B-5)
6911 S University Boulevard (Southglenn Mall - North end), Centennial
Farmers' Market Hotline: 303-887-FARM
www.denverfarmersmarket.com
Late June - Late October
Tuesday, 10 a.m. - 4 p.m.

Cherry Creek Fresh Market   (B-5)
1st Avenue and University (Bed, Bath & Beyond parking lot), Denver
303-442-1837
Early June - Late September
Wednesday, 9 a.m. - 1 p.m.
Early May - Late October
Saturday, 7:30 a.m. - 12:30 p.m.

City Park Esplanade Fresh Market   (B-5)
City Park Esplanade between 17th and Colfax (by East High School), Denver
303-442-1837
Early June - Late October
Sunday, 9 a.m. - 1 p.m.

The Evergreen Farmers' Market   (B-5)
I-70 exit at Evergreen Parkway (In the Evergreen Wal-Mart parking lot)
Colorado Mountain Markets
303-421-2076
Early June - Mid-October
Tuesday, 10 a.m. - 2 p.m.

Flatiron Crossing Farmers' Market   (B-4)
In The Village, Flatiron Crossing Mall, Broomfield
720-887-7467 or 303-570-FARM
www.coloradofarmersmarket.com
June - October
Thursday, 3 p.m. - 9 p.m.
Saturday, 10 a.m. - 3 p.m

Golden Farmers' Market   (B-5)
Jackson between 12th and 13th Streets, downtown Golden
303-932-6884
email: jamladycolorado@aol.com
Early June - Early September
Saturday, 8 a.m. - 12 p.m.

Historic Olde Town Arvada Farmers' Market   (B-5)
7212 Ralston Road (1 block west of Wadsworth Bypass between Teller and Upham), Arvada
303-420-6100
www.historicarvada.org
Early June - Late October
Thursday, 8 a.m. - 2 p.m.

Littleton Farmers' Market   (C-5)
Broadway and Ridge Road (Aspen Grove Lifestyle Center), Littleton
Farmers' Market Hotline 303-887-FARM
www.denverfarmersmarket.com
Late June - Late October
Wednesday, 11 a.m.- sellout

Longmont Farmers' Market   (B-5)
North Lot, Boulder County Fairgrounds (near Colorado Road & Boston Avenue), Longmont
www.longmontfarmer.com
Early July- Late August
Tuesday, 9 p.m. – 1p.m.
Mid-May - Late October
Saturday, 8 a.m.- 1 p.m.

The Market at Sloans Lake   (B-5)
25th Street and Sheridan, Denver
Mid-June - Late September
Thursday, 9 a.m. –2 p.m.

Northglenn Farmers' Market   (B-5)
104th and I-25 (Northglenn Market Place), Northglenn
Farmers' Market Hotline: 303-887-FARM
www.denverfarmersmarket.com
Late June - Late October
Saturday, 8 a.m. - sellout

Old South Pearl Street Farmers' Market   (B-5)
On the 1500 block of South Pearl Street, Denver
303-232-2935
Mid-June - Late September
Sunday, 10 a.m. - 2 p.m

Plum Creek Valley Farmers' Market   (C-5)
100 Wilcox Street, Castle Rock
720-733-6930
email: dcsue@douglas.co.us
Mid-July - Early October
Saturday, 8 a.m. - 12 p.m.

South Aurora Farmers' Market   (B-6)
15324 E. Hampden Circle, Aurora
303-361-6169
email: Daurorabus@aol.com
www.AuroraBusiness.org
Mid-July - First Frost
Wednesday, 7 a.m. - sellout

Southwest Plaza Farmers' Market   (B-5)
W. Bowles and S. Wadsworth, Littleton
Farmers' Market Hotline: 303-887-FARM
www.denverfarmersmarket.com
Early June - Late October
Saturday, 8 a.m.

Strasburg Community Council Farmers' Market   (B-7)
Lucky Strike Bowling Lane Parking Lot, Strasburg
303-622-9588
email: pattyjaned@tds.com
Late June- Late August
Saturday, 7 a.m. - 11 a.m.

Union Station Farmers Market   (B-5)
17th and Wynkoop (LoDo), downtown Denver
Farmers' Market Hotline: 303-887-FARM
www.denverfarmersmarket.com
Late June - Late October
Sunday, 8 a.m. – 1 p.m.

Villa Italia Mall Farmers' Market   (B-5)
W. Alameda and Wadsworth, Lakewood
Farmers' Market Hotline: 303-887-FARM
www.denverfarmersmarket.com
Late June - Late October
Thursday, 11 a.m. – sellout

Westminster Farmers' Market   (B-5)
3295 W. 72nd Avenue (Community Senior Center), Westminster
303-475-3062
email: penny@pennysantiques.com
Mid-June - Late September
Thursday, 9 a.m. - 2 p.m.

Westminster Market Place   (B-5)
105th and Sheridan (Westminster Park)
Farmers' Market Hotline: 303-570-FARM
www.coloradofarmersmarket.com
Early June - October
Sunday, 10 a.m. - 4 p.m.

Northeast
Estes Valley Farmers' Market   (A-4)
470 Prospect Village Drive (Next to the Estes Park Brewery), Estes Park
970-586-7166
email: eeandrnlewis@aol.com
Early June - Late September
Thursday, 8 a.m. - 12:30 p.m.

Fort Collins Farmers' Market   (A-4)
2201 S. College Avenue (Old Ward's parking lot), Fort Collins
Farmers' Market Hotline: 303-570-FARM
www.coloradofarmersmarket.com
May - October
Wednesday and Sunday, call for times

Fort Collins Farmers' Market   (A-4)
802 W. Drake, Fort Collins
970-495-4889
June - October
Wednesday, 2 p.m. - 6 p.m.
May - October
Sunday, 11 a.m. - 3 p.m.
Northeast corner of Lincoln and 5th Street, Loveland
970-495-4889
July - Late October
Tuesday, 2 p.m. - 6 p.m.

Greeley Farmers' Market at the Depot   (A-6)
902 7th Avenue, Greeley
970-350-9783
July - October
Wednesday, 4 p.m. - 6 p.m.
Saturday, 7:30 a.m. - 11 a.m.

Larimer County Master Gardeners' Farmers' Market   (A-6)
1525 Blue Spruce Drive (Old Town Fort Collins at Olive and Remington), Fort Collins
970-498-6000
email: rtolan@larimer.org
Early July - Late September
Saturday, 8 a.m. - 12 p.m.

Windsor Farmers' Market @Pioneer Village Museum   (A-6)
116 N. 5th Street (Boardwalk Park and Pioneer Village Museum), Windsor
970-686-6404
email: generalstore@earthlink.net
Mid-July - September
Thursday, 4 p.m. - 7 p.m.

Northwest

Minturn Summer Market   (C-4)
Town of Minturn
970-827-9502
Mid-June - Mid-September
Saturday, 9 a.m. - 2 p.m.

Town of Dillon Farmers' Market   (C-4)
PO Box 8 (Lake Dillon Marina Parking Lot), Dillon
970-262-3403
Late June - Late September
Friday, 9 a.m. - 1 p.m.

Vail Farmers' Market   (C-4)
Meadow Drive at Vail Village Inn Plaza, Vail
Farmers' Market Hotline: 303-570-FARM
www.coloradofarmersmarket.com
June - September
Sunday, 10 a.m. - 4 p.m.

Southeast

Colorado Springs Farmers' Market   (D-6)
Memorial Park, Colorado Springs
719-574-1283
July - Early October
Thursday, 7 a.m. - 1:30 p.m.
24th Street and W. Colorado Avenue, Colorado Springs
Mid-June - Mid-October
Saturday, 7 a.m. - 1:30 p.m.
4515 Barnes Road, Colorado Springs
Mid-June - Mid-October
Saturday, 7 a.m. - 1:30 p.m.

Pueblo Farmers' Marketeers   (E-6)
Midtown Shopping Center, Pueblo
719-583-6566
Early July - Mid-October
Tuesday and Friday, 7 a.m. - 1 p.m.

Trinidad - Las Animas County Farmers' Market   (G-6)
134 W. Main, Trinidad
Late June - Late September
Saturday, 8 a.m. - 1 p.m.

Teller County Farmers' Market f Association   (D-6)
PO Box 464, West Street (Kavanagh parking area), Woodland Park
719-689-2503 or 719-689-3133
Late June - Mid-September
Friday, 7 a.m. - 1 p.m.

Southwest

Fremont County Farmers' Market   (E-5)
Gibson's Discount Center parking lot, Canon City
719-269-7683
Mid-June - September
Wednesday, 2 p.m. - 6:30 p.m.

Durango Farmers' Market   (G-2)
259 W. 9th Street (9th Street City Car Park), Durango
970-247-4355 ext. 234
Mid-July - October
Wednesday, 4:30 p.m. - 7 p.m.
1st National Bank parking lot
Early June - Mid-October
Saturday, 8 a.m. - 12 p.m.

Montezuma County Farmers' Market   (G-1)
109 W. Main Street (Courthouse parking lot, south side of Main Street), Cortez
970-565-3123
Late June - Early October
Saturday, 7:30 a.m. - 12 p.m.

Ridgway Farmers' Market   (E-2)
Ouray County Fairgrounds (U.S. Hwy 550, just south of Ridgway's only stoplight), Ouray
970-626-9775
email: jbennett@co.ouray.co.us
Early June - Late September
Sunday, 8 a.m. - 12 p.m.

Uncompahgre Farmers' Market   (E-2)
S. First Street at Centennial Plaza, Montrose
970-240-9498
Mid-June - September
Wednesday, 8:30 a.m. - 12:30 p.m.
May - October
Saturday, 8:30 a.m. - 12:30 p.m.

Contributor Index

Bill and Phyllis Roth Farms
2210 Fern Avenue
Greeley, CO 80631
970-352-5409
email: paroth43@cs.com

Bingham Hill Cheese Company
1716 Heath Parkway
Fort Collins, CO 80524
970-472-0702
email: tom@binghamhill.com
www.binghamhill.com

Blue Point Bakery
1721 E 58 Ave.
Denver, CO 80216
303-298-1100

Boulder Cork
3295 30th Street
Boulder, CO 80302
303-443-9505

Braddy's Downtown Restaurant
160 W. Oak
Fort Collins, CO 80525
970-498-0873
email: info@braddys.com
www.braddys.com

Buffalo Groves, Inc.
PO Box 900
Kiowa Colorado 80117
303-621-1111
email: info@buffalogroves.com
www.buffalogroves.com

Burke Organic Farms
PO Box 19813
Boulder, CO 80308
303-442-1837
email: freshmarkets@qwest.com

Canino's Sausage Co., Inc.
4414 Jason Street
Denver, CO 80211
303-455-4339 / 800-538-0148
email: comments@caninosausage.com
www.caninosausage.com

César Flores
191 University Boulevard. #118
Denver, CO 80206
303-529-7211
email: cesarflor@yahoo.com

Claire de Lune
1313 East 6th Avenue
Denver, CO 80218
303-831-1992

Coleman Natural Products
5140 Race Court
Denver, Colorado 80216
800-442-8666
email: Coleman@ColemanNatural.com
www.colemanbeef.com

Colorado Beef Council
789 Sherman Street, Suite 105
Denver, CO 80203
303-830-7892
email: info@cobeef.com
www.cobeef.com

Colorado Elk and Game Meats
72015 Kinikin Road
Montrose, CO 81401
877-970-4329
email: Info@Colorado-Elk.com
www.colorado-elk.com

Colorado Farmers Market Association
3889 75th
Boulder, CO 80301
phone and fax: 303-440-0750
email: farmerjde@idcomm.com

Colorado Potato Administrative Committee
PO Box 348
Monte Vista, CO 81144
719-852-3322
email: office@coloradopotato.org
www.coloradopotato.org

Cook Street School of Fine Cooking
1937 Market Street
Denver, CO 80202
303-308-9300
email: info@cookstreet.com
www.cookstreet.com

Cooking School of the Rockies
637-H South Broadway
Boulder, CO 80304
303-494-7988 / 877-249-0305
www.cookingschoolrockies.com

Cotswold Cottage Foods, Ltd.
14005 Dogleg Lane
Broomfield, CO 80020
720-887-4771 / 888-208-1977
email: cotswoldcottage@worldnet.att.net

Cuisine Catering
PO Box 1056
Avon, CO 81620
970-926-4986

Denver Urban Gardens
3377 Blake Street, Suite 113
Denver, CO 80205
Phone: 303.292.9900
email: dirt@dug.org
www.dug.org

Eden Valley Farm
6263 NCR 29
Loveland, CO 80538
970-622-0418
email: feedback@eden-valley.org
www.eden-valley.org

Ela Family Farms
3075 L Road
Hotchkiss, CO 81419
970-872-3488
email: sela@co.tds.net

First Fruits Organic Farms
PO Box 864
Paonia, CO 81428
970-527-6122

Fourth Story
2955 E. First Avenue (Tattered Cover)
Denver, CO 80206
303-322-1824
reservations@tatteredcover.com
www.tatteredcover.com

The Fresh Herb Company
4114 Oxford Road
Longmont, CO
303-449-5994

Front Range Organic Gardeners
Dona Erickson
55 S. Lincoln, #209
Denver, CO 80209
303-282-4821
email: derickson@IN2L.com

Full Moon Grill
2525 Arapahoe Avenue
Arapahoe Village Shopping Center
Boulder CO 80302
303-938-8800

Grande Premium Elk Meat
19612 W. State Hwy. 160
Del Norte, CO 81132
719-657-0942 / 888-338-4581
email: jan@uselk.com
303-938-8800

Grant Family Farms
1020 WCR 72
Wellington, CO 80549
970-568-7645
email: jimyoung@grantfarms.com
www.grantfarms.com

Grassmick Produce & Coins
30017 CR 17
Rocky Ford, CO 81607
719-254-3047
email: grassmick@centurytel.net
www.grassmickcoins.com

Green Earth Farms
PO Box 672 / 65 N. 8th Street
Saguache, CO 81149
719-655-2655
www.greenearthfarm.com

Gwin Farms
14377 County Road #13
Platteville, CO 80651
970-535-0720

Haystack Mountain Goat Dairy
5239 Niwot Road
Niwot, CO 80503
303-581-9948
email: info@haystackgoatcheese.com
www.haystackgoatcheese.com

Heine's Market
11801 West 44th Avenue
Wheat Ridge, CO
303-425-9955

J&J Apiaries
2936 Garrett Drive
Fort Collins, CO 80526
970-204-6754
email: jandjapiaries@frii.com

Kelley Bean
101 Main St.
Ovid, CO 80744
970-463-5468

La Tour Restaurant
122 E. Meadow Drive
Vail, CO 81657
970-476-4403
email: latour@qwest.net
www.latour-vail.com

Loredana's Pesto
5701 Yukon Street
Arvada, CO 80002
303-421-2076
email: loredanaspesto@aol.com

Maggie McCullough's Bread Shop
116 East Foothills Parkway, #5
Fort Collins, CO 80525
970-282-8460

Mattics Orchards
8163 High Mesa Road
Olathe, Colorado 81425.
970-323-5281

Maverick Ranch
5360 Franklin Street
Denver, CO 80216
www.maverickranch.com

McCurry Farms
2981 West 144th Avenue
Broomfield, CO 80020
303-947-8839

Monroe Organic Farms
25525 WCR 48
Kersey, CO 80644
970-284-7941
email: jacquie@monroefarm.com
www.monroefarm.com

Morrison's Back Acker
33 Alles Drive
Greeley, CO80631
970-356-4470

Munson Farms
714 Topaz Street
Superior, CO 80027
303-543-9958
email: mmunson@us.ibm.com

New West Foods
1120 Lincoln Street, Suite 905
Denver, CO 80203
800-831-1292
www.newwestfoods.com

Osborn Farm
1933 S.E. 14th
Loveland, CO 80537
970-669-4407
email: osborn1861@aol.com

Palisade Peach Fest
Palisade, CO
www.palisadepeachfest.com
email: info@palisadepeachfest.com

Pastures of Plenty
4039 Ogallala Road
Longmont, CO 80301
303-440-5220

Potager
1109 Ogden
Denver, CO 80218
303-861-8985

Princess Beef
3150 D Road
Crawford, CO 81415
970-921-7821
email: CynthRanch@aol.com

Pueblo Farmers Marketeers
Pueblo, CO
719-583-6566

Q's Restaurant
Boulderado Hotel, 2115 13th Street
Boulder, CO 80302
303-444-5232

R&K Farms
29920 MCR-H
Brush, CO 80723
970-842-0926

Restaurant six89
689 Main Street
Carbondale, Colorado.
970.963.6890
www.six89.com

Rock Creek Farm
2005 S. 112th Street
Broomfield, CO 80020
303-465-9565
email: Megan@rockcreekfarm.com
rockcreekfarm.com

Seasoned Chef Cooking School
999 Jasmine Street, Suite 100
Denver, CO 80220
303-377-3222
email: info@theseasonedchef.com
www.theseasonedchef.com

Straw Hat Farm
66839 Solar Road
Montrose, CO 81401
970-240-6163

Sunshine Farms
227 Rodman Lane
Durango, CO 81303
970-259-7595
email: sunshinefarm01@hotmail.com

Tigges Farm
12404 Weld County Road 64
Greeley, CO 80631
970-686-7863
email: ckrickart@cs.com

Tony's Meats and Specialty Foods
4991 E. Dry Creek Road
Littleton, Colorado, 80122
303-770-7024
www.tonysmarket.com
(3 Denver area locations)

Wholesome Harvest Farm
4773 C.R. 514
Ignacio, CO 81137
970-886-0437

Willow River Cheese Importers
33 South Pratt Parkway
Longmont, CO
303-443-4444

Colorado Crop Calendar

May	June	July	Aug	Sept	Oct	Nov

apples (storage to June1)

apricots

asparagus

beets

bell peppers

broccoli

cabbage

cantaloupe

carrots

cauliflower

celery

cherries

chile peppers

cucumbers

eggplant

grapes

green beans

herbs

honeydew

lettuce (leaf and head)

onions (to March 15, storage included)

peaches

pears

pinto beans (year-round)

plums

popcorn (year-round)

potatoes (year-round)

pumpkins

raspberries

rhubarb

squash

strawberries

sweet corn

tomatoes

watermelon

Courtesy of the Colorado Department of Agriculture

Index

3D Press Book Catalog

Boulder Cooks
Recipes and Profiles from Boulder County's Best Kitchens
$18.95 / 204pp / 0-9634607-8-1

Denver Hiking Guide
45 Hikes within 45 Minutes of Denver.
$12.95 / 104pp / ISBN 1-889593-58-3

Colorado Bed & Breakfast Cookbook
From the Warmth & Hospitality of 88 Colorado B&B's and Country Inns
$19.95 / 320pp / 0-9653751-0-2

Colorado Farmers' Market Cookbook
200 Recipes Fresh From Colorado's Farmers' Markets & Chefs
$18.95 / 224 pp / ISBN 1-889593-00-1

Colorado Month-to-Month Gardening
A Practical Guide for Designing, Growing and Maintaining Your Colorado Garden
$19.95 / 162pp / ISBN 1-889593-01-X

Month-to-Month Gardening Utah
Tips for Designing, Growing and Maintaining Your Utah Garden
$16.95 / 162pp / ISBN 1-889593-03-6

Month-to-Month Gardening New Mexico
Tips for Designing, Growing and Maintaining Your New Mexico Garden
$16.95 / ISBN 1-889593-02-8 / $16.95

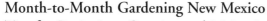

Washington State Bed & Breakfast
From the Warmth & Hospitality of 85 B&B's and Country Inns throughout Washington State.
$21.95 / ISBN 0-9653751-9-6 / 320pp

3D Press Order Form

4340 E. KENTUCKY AVE., Suite 446
DENVER, CO 80246
888-456-3607

PLEASE SEND ME:	Price	Quantity
BOULDER COOKS	$18.95	_____
COLORADO BED & BREAKFAST COOKBOOK	$19.95	_____
COLORADO FARMERS' MARKET COOKBOOK	$18.95	_____
COLORADO MONTH-TO-MONTH GARDENING	$19.95	_____
DENVER HIKING GUIDE	$12.95	_____
MONTH-TO-MONTH GARDENING UTAH	$16.95	_____
MONTH-TO-MONTH GARDENING NEW MEXICO	$16.95	_____
WASHINGTON BED & BREAKFAST COOKBOOK	$21.95	_____

SUBTOTAL: $ _____

Colorado residents add 3.8% sales tax. $ _____

Add $5.00 for shipping for 1st book, add $1 for each additional $ _____

TOTAL ENCLOSED: $ _____

SEND TO:

Name _____

Address_____

City _____State _____Zip _____

Gift From _____

We accept checks, money orders, Visa or Mastercard (please include expiration date). Please make checks payable to 3D Press, Inc. Sorry, no COD orders.

Please charge my ☐ VISA ☐ MASTERCARD

Card Number _____ Expiration Date _____

Cardholder's Signature _____

CALL TOLL FREE 888-456-3607 FOR MORE INFORMATION

3D Press Book Catalog

Boulder Cooks
Recipes and Profiles from Boulder County's Best Kitchens
$18.95 / 204pp / 0-9634607-8-1

Denver Hiking Guide
45 Hikes within 45 Minutes of Denver.
$12.95 / 104pp / ISBN 1-889593-58-3

Colorado Bed & Breakfast Cookbook
From the Warmth & Hospitality of 88 Colorado B&B's and Country Inns
$19.95 / 320pp / 0-9653751-0-2

Colorado Farmers' Market Cookbook
200 Recipes Fresh From Colorado's Farmers' Markets & Chefs
$18.95 / 224 pp / ISBN 1-889593-00-1

Colorado Month-to-Month Gardening
A Practical Guide for Designing, Growing and Maintaining Your Colorado Garden
$19.95 / 162pp / ISBN 1-889593-01-X

Month-to-Month Gardening Utah
Tips for Designing, Growing and Maintaining Your Utah Garden
$16.95 / 162pp / ISBN 1-889593-03-6

Month-to-Month Gardening New Mexico
Tips for Designing, Growing and Maintaining Your New Mexico Garden
$16.95 / ISBN 1-889593-02-8 / $16.95

Washington State Bed & Breakfast
From the Warmth & Hospitality of 85 B&B's and Country Inns throughout Washington State.
$21.95 / ISBN 0-9653751-9-6 / 320pp

3D Press Order Form

4340 E. KENTUCKY AVE., Suite 446
DENVER, CO 80246
888-456-3607

PLEASE SEND ME:	Price	Quantity
BOULDER COOKS	$18.95	_____
COLORADO BED & BREAKFAST COOKBOOK	$19.95	_____
COLORADO FARMERS' MARKET COOKBOOK	$18.95	_____
COLORADO MONTH-TO-MONTH GARDENING	$19.95	_____
DENVER HIKING GUIDE	$12.95	_____
MONTH-TO-MONTH GARDENING UTAH	$16.95	_____
MONTH-TO-MONTH GARDENING NEW MEXICO	$16.95	_____
WASHINGTON BED & BREAKFAST COOKBOOK	$21.95	_____

SUBTOTAL: $ _____

Colorado residents add 3.8% sales tax. $ _____

Add $5.00 for shipping for 1st book, add $1 for each additional $ _____

TOTAL ENCLOSED: $ _____

SEND TO:

Name _____

Address_____

City _____State _____Zip _____

Gift From _____

We accept checks, money orders, Visa or Mastercard (please include expiration date). Please make checks payable to 3D Press, Inc. Sorry, no COD orders.

Please charge my   ☐ VISA   ☐ MASTERCARD

Card Number _____ Expiration Date _____

Cardholder's Signature _____

CALL TOLL FREE 888-456-3607 FOR MORE INFORMATION